The Costs and Benefits of Large-scale Immigration

The Costs and Benefits of Large-scale Immigration

Exploring the economic and demographic consequences for the UK

Robert Rowthorn

CIVITAS

First Published December 2015

55 Tufton Street
London SW1P 3QL

email: books@civitas.org.uk

ISBN 978-1-906837-74-7

Designed and typeset by
lukejefford.com

Printed in Great Britain by
Berforts Group Ltd
Stevenage, SGI 2BH

Contents

Author

Robert Rowthorn is Emeritus Professor of Economics at the University of Cambridge and Fellow of King's College. He is the author of several books including De-industrialisation and Foreign Trade (with John Wells) and academic articles on economic growth, structural change, employment and migration. He has been a consultant to the International Monetary Fund, the UN Commission on Trade and Development and the International Labour Organisation, as well as to British government departments and a variety of private sector firms and organisations.

Acknowledgements

I should like to thank Sir Andrew Green, David Green, Mervyn Stone, Brian Van Arkadie and Nigel Williams for helpful comments on various drafts of this book.

Preface

The issue of immigration has been thrown into sharp relief by the current Syrian refugee crisis and by the huge flows of migrants from many different countries travelling thousands of miles, and risking their lives, for the chance of a better life in the EU. Every day the media are full of images of drowned children, rescued families, and streams of migrants heading for Germany. The scale of recent migration has taken Europeans by surprise and their leaders are desperately seeking to improvise a collective policy to reduce this flow. Such a policy can only work with the active collaboration of Turkey and the countries of North Africa. Without their support it will be difficult within accepted moral and legal constraints to reduce significantly the flow of migrants entering the EU through these countries.

The proximate causes of recent flows are the inability of Libya to control the departure of migrants from its shores and the refusal of Turkey to do so. The current negotiations are intended to bring Turkey on board, but the post-Gaddafi regime in Libya is too weak to help much even if it wanted to. The deeper causes of current migrant flows are the conflicts in Afghanistan, Eritrea and the Middle East, together with the large disparity in economic and social conditions between the EU and much of Africa, the Middle East and beyond. Only when these conflicts are resolved and the gap in living standards is greatly reduced will migration pressure ease.

How long the conflicts will last is a matter of speculation, but one thing is certain: it will take many years to bring in living standards in poor countries to the point where there is no economic incentive for large-scale migration.

The present situation raises many moral and practical questions for the UK. To what extent can we or should we limit the flow of non-EU migrants into this country? How far should we collaborate with other EU countries on migration policy and how far should we go it alone? What criteria should we use for granting asylum or permitting the entry of economic migrants? To what extent should the interests of migrants and their countries of origin be reflected in these criteria? These are questions that have concerned me for a number of years, although I have written very little about them.

The main focus of my work on migration has been on the economic and demographic impact of immigration on advanced economies, in particular the UK. This is also the focus of the present book, although in the concluding chapter I make some provisional observations about moral and political aspects of migration policy. I hope to address these wider issues in depth in a later work, but for the moment in this book I restrict myself mainly to what I know best. This book is an updated version of an earlier online paper on immigration that I wrote for Civitas.[1] In producing this version I have kept alterations to a minimum. I have updated the statistics where feasible and in a few places I have modified the text in the light of recent developments, but that is all.

Robert Rowthorn
King's College, Cambridge
October 2015
rer3@econ.cam.ac.uk

Overview

This book is about the consequences of large-scale immigration. Immigration on the scale the UK has experienced in recent years has many potential consequences. If it persists over a long period of time, it may radically alter the cultural, ethnic, racial and political character of this country.[1] It may be disruptive and undermine social cohesion, with negative implications for national identity and democratic governance. It may also bring benefits such as a more varied cuisine, exposure to new ideas and a less parochial world-view amongst the native population. I have written elsewhere on these issues (Rowthorn, 2003) and they have been discussed recently in depth by David Goodhart (2012) and Paul Collier (2013). I have little to add to what they say on the cultural and related aspects of immigration. Apart from some general observations in the closing chapter, this book is almost exclusively concerned with the economic and demographic consequences of migration. My focus is mainly on the UK although I do occasionally draw on international evidence. I have tried to be objective, but like anyone else my evaluation of the evidence is shaped by my prior beliefs. Sources for most of the graphs and tables are given in Appendix 2.

The main conclusions of the book are as follows:

- Net migration into the UK from the EU is currently around 180,000 per annum. The future scale of such migration will depend on what happens to the economies of eastern and southern Europe. Poland and the Baltic states are expected to grow quite fast and the migration of workers to the UK from these countries should begin to fall in the near future, although there is no sign of this happening yet. Net migration from southern Europe and from Bulgaria and Romania is likely to remain at a high level for some years to come.

- If net migration from the EU continues at anything like the present rate, it will be impossible to achieve David Cameron's target of net migration 'in the tens of thousands'.
- In almost every year over the past decade, net migration has been higher than the rate of 225,000 per annum assumed by the Office for National Statistics (ONS) in its high migration projection. Net migration in the latest year for which figures are available was 330,000.
- Taking into account the children born to future migrants, with net migration at the rate envisaged under the ONS high migration scenario (225,000 p.a.), the UK population would increase by a projected 20 million over the next 50 years and by 29 million over the next 75 years. This growth would be almost entirely due to migration.
- Assuming the extra workers were productively employed, the result would be an appreciably faster growth in total GDP than would otherwise be the case. The effect on GDP per capita would be marginal.
- Net migration at the rate envisaged under the ONS high migration scenario would have a rejuvenating effect on the national population and increase the share of this population who are of working age.

However, these benefits would be modest and once achieved they could only be maintained through a continued high rate of net migration into the indefinite future.

- The economic gains from large-scale immigration come mainly from its impact on the age structure of the population. Most of these gains could be achieved with a much lower rate of net migration, and hence a much lower rate of population growth, than the UK is currently experiencing.
- The age structure is conveniently summarised by the dependency ratio (the number of persons aged 65+ per 100 persons aged 15-64). With net migration of 225,000 p.a. the ONS projects that the dependency ratio would increase to 50.5% by 2087 and the population would reach 92.9 million. With net migration of 50,000 p.a., the dependency ratio in 2087 would be 54.0% and the population 74.2 million. Comparing the two scenarios, the extra migration required to reduce the 2087 dependency ratio by 3.5 percentage points (from 54.0% to 50.5%) adds an extra 18.7 million to the national population. To maintain this modest benefit would require continued net migration at the higher rate in perpetuity.
- Dustmann and Frattini (2013a) estimate that the migrant population as a whole generated a fiscal surplus of between -0.5% and +0.2% of GDP over the period 2001-2011. They also estimate that over this period recent migrants from the European Economic Area (EEA) generated a fiscal surplus of between £22 billion and £36 billion. These estimates are probably too high. However, even after plausible downward adjustments, it seems likely that recent EEA migrants have either paid their way or generated a modest surplus.

- Immigration from outside the EEA is estimated by the official Migration Advisory Committee to have had a negative impact on the level of native employment in the years immediately following the financial crisis of 2007-8. The same is probably true of immigration from within the EEA, although the statistical evidence on this point is less solid.
- Unskilled workers have suffered some reduction in their wages due to competition from immigrants.
- Even on optimistic assumptions, the economic and fiscal gains for existing inhabitants and their descendants from large-scale immigration are small in comparison to its impact on population growth.
- Government policy towards immigration from outside the EU is becoming more selective, making it difficult for unskilled workers to enter, but encouraging the entry of skilled and talented individuals.
- If this policy is applied systematically to poor countries it may denude them of the professional elites upon which they depend.
- Controls over migration from poor countries should be designed in such a way as to promote their welfare and economic development. Migration policy towards these countries should be seen as a complement to the official aid policy and not as a means of enriching ourselves at their expense.

The structure of the book is as follows. Chapter 1 gives an overview of modern migration into and out of the UK. Chapter 2 considers the labour market impact of migration. Chapter 3 considers the influence of migration on population growth and age structure. It also considers the advantages and disadvantages of population growth. Chapter 4 considers at length the impact of migration on government finances. The book ends with some conclusions and some general observations on migration policy.

1

Recent UK migration

The number of immigrants in the UK population has grown rapidly over the past 20 years. In 1991 there were 4.9 million residents who were born abroad. By 2014 this had risen to 8.3 million, of whom 4.8 million were employed.

Every year millions of people enter or leave the United Kingdom. Most of them are tourists or other short-term visitors. Some are long-term migrants. Official UK statistics define an international long-term migrant as 'someone who changes his or her country of usual residence for a period of at least a year, so that the country of destination effectively becomes the country of usual residence'. The inflow of long-term migrants is normally described as 'immigration' and the outflow as 'emigration'.

Table 1.1 summarises UK experience with regard to long-term migration since 1991. The data in this table classify migrants by country of birth. The main points to note are as follows:

- Over the period 1991-2013 as a whole, it is estimated that 10.6 million long-term migrants entered the UK and 7.3 million left. Thus, estimated inflows exceeded outflows by 3.3 million. Following the 2011 Census, the ONS has revised its estimate for net migration upwards to 3.7 million for the period 1991-2013.[1]
- The number of UK-born individuals leaving this country during the period 1991-2013 was twice as

large as the number of returnees. As a result, there was a net outflow of 1.6 million natives over the period.

- During this period 8.8 million foreign-born individuals entered the UK and only 3.9 million left. As a result, there was a net inflow of 4.9 million foreign-born migrants.
- The disparity between inflows and outflows was greatest for the mostly poor countries in the columns labelled 'New Commonwealth' (mainly countries in Africa and South Asia) and 'Other Foreign'.
- The scale of immigration increased considerably when Labour came to power in 1997 and relaxed immigration controls.

Table 1.1: Long-term UK migration flows by country of birth 1991-2013 (thousands)

	All countries	UK	EU15	EU8	Old Common-wealth	New Common-wealth	Other foreign
Inflow							
1991-1997	2135	561	414	:	185	422	553
1998-2013	8496	1243	1125	786	850	1871	2621
Total	10631	1804	1539	786	1035	2293	3174
Outflow							
1991-1997	1849	952	315	:	137	145	300
1998-2013	5465	2436	756	316	525	463	969
Total	7314	3388	1071	316	662	608	1269
Balance							
1991-1997	286	-391	98	:	49	277	254
1998-2013	3031	1193	369	470	325	1408	1652
Total	3317	1584	468	470	373	1685	1905

Country groupings are as follows. EU15: Austria, Belgium, Denmark, Finland, France, Germany, Greece, Republic of Ireland, Italy, Luxembourg, Netherlands, Portugal, Spain and Sweden. EU8: Czech Republic, Estonia, Hungary, Latvia, Lithuania, Poland, Slovakia and Slovenia. Migrants born in the UK are excluded from all EU groupings and are shown separately. 'Other foreign' includes the EU8 countries before 2004. Bulgaria and Romania are classified as 'other foreign' throughout. Note that totals may not add up because of rounding errors.

Figure 1.1: Net migration of non-British citizens 2004–2015 (rolling 12 month totals, thousands)

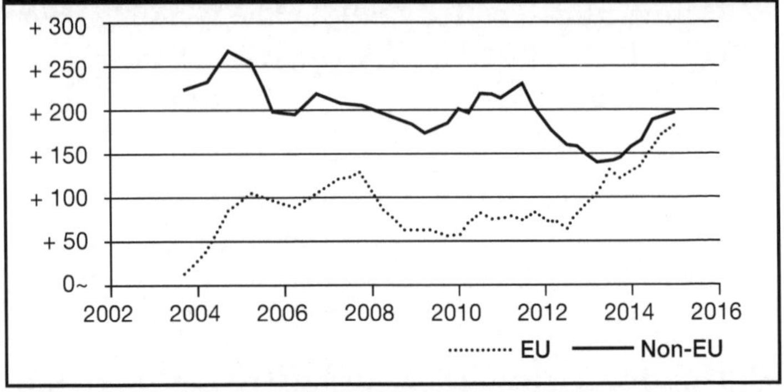

Figure 1.2: Net migration by citizenship 2004–2015 (rolling 12 month totals, thousands)

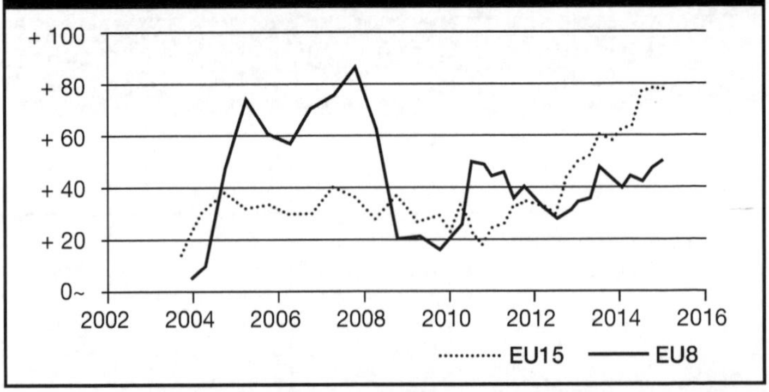

Figure 1.3: Net migration of non-EU citizens 2004–2015 (rolling 12 month totals, thousands)

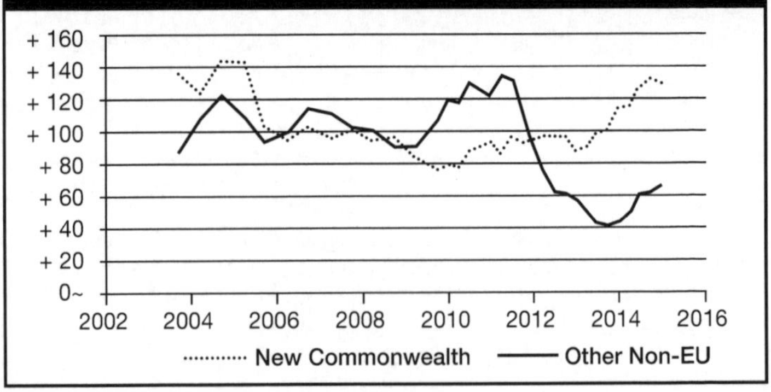

- Net migration from non-EU countries has historically been greater than net migration from the EU. However, the gap has recently diminished following new restrictions on non-EU immigration and an upsurge of immigration from the EU, in particular southern Europe, Bulgaria and Romania. Net migration (inflow minus outflow) from the EU is now only slightly less than from the rest of the world combined (Figure 1.1).[2] The reduction in net migration from outside the EU is accounted for by a sharp fall in net migration from the New Commonwealth (Figure 1.3), due partly to a clamp-down on so-called 'bogus' students from these countries.
- Historical migration patterns are reflected in official population statistics. In 2013, the 10 most common countries of origin amongst foreign-born residents of the UK were: India (760,000), Poland (688,000), Pakistan (516,000), Republic of Ireland (378,000), Germany (297,000), Bangladesh (228,000), South Africa (221,000), USA (197,000), China (191,000) and Nigeria (185,000).[3]

Economic factors are the main driving force behind these various flows. Per capita income and wages in the UK are still many times greater than in much of Africa and South Asia. They are also well above the level in some ex-communist countries. Wages are still relatively high in southern Europe for those fortunate enough to have a job, but in the wake of the financial crisis there is now widespread unemployment especially amongst younger people. Such differences provide a powerful incentive for migration. Even where the reason for migration is not ostensibly economic, as in the case of marriage or asylum, the decision of where to settle down may be influenced by economic considerations. For example, if a person from a rich country marries someone from a poor country, the couple may choose to settle in the rich country because it offers better economic prospects.[4] Or, as the Syrian crisis illustrates, people fleeing conflict may initially find refuge in a neighbouring poor country but then move on to a richer country where life is better. They will continue to be officially classified as refugees although the motivation for the later stages of their odyssey may be mainly economic.

Figure 1.4 summarises the ONS data on national insurance number registration by EU nationals. These indicate the scale of work-related migration. The main developments over the past decade are as follows. Since the financial crisis in 2007-8, there has been an upsurge in work-related migration from southern Europe. There has also been a recent upsurge in work-related migration from Bulgaria and Romania. Finally, despite a sharp fall following the financial crisis, work-related migration from the remaining former communist countries has remained at a fairly high level. Together these developments explain why net migration from the EU is currently so high.

Figure 1.4: National Insurance number registrations for nationals from selected EU countries 2002–2014 (thousands)

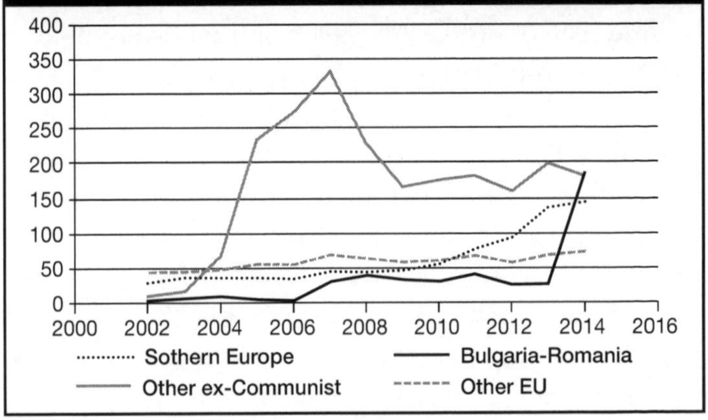

The impact of the financial crisis on southern Europe can be gauged from the unemployment statistics. Unemployment rates for people aged 15-24 in 2014 were: Italy 42.7%, Portugal 34.7%, Spain 53.2% and Greece 52.4%.[5] Job opportunities rather than wage differentials are the main incentive for young people from these countries to migrate to the UK. Even on the most optimistic assumptions, it will take some years for unemployment in these countries to fall to the point where it is no longer a major incentive for outward migration.

Following the collapse of communism, the countries of eastern Europe experienced a severe economic contraction. This was followed by a period of recovery during which per capita incomes grew much faster than in the UK. However, the financial crisis hit a number of these countries hard and their growth rates have not fully recovered. Per capita incomes in the larger ex-communist countries in 2014 were still relatively low compared to the UK: Bulgaria 42%, Romania 50%, Hungary 63% and Poland 63%.[6] However, the gap is closing and if this process continues the incentive for large-scale migration will eventually disappear. The Polish ambassador to the UK has claimed that the 'wave' of large-scale Polish migration to the UK has come to an end.[7] This is not borne out by official statistics which indicate that national insurance number registrations by Polish nationals have increased during the UK economic recovery.[8] Still, the ambassador does have a point. He is just a little premature. The Polish economy is growing rapidly and the incentive for outward migration should soon diminish.

One striking development has been the surge in immigration from Bulgaria and Romania since the lifting of work restrictions on 1 January 2014. The rate of immigration from these countries has risen from around

10,000 p.a. in 2011-2012 to 53,000 in the year ending March 2015.[9] The scale of the increase is exaggerated in the data shown in Figure 1.4, where the very large figure for 2014 includes national insurance number registration by workers who were already in the country when the year began. Given the relatively low wages and per capita incomes in Bulgaria and Romania it is likely that immigration on a large scale from these countries will continue for some years.

Fertility and age structure

Immigration has a direct impact on the size of the national population. It also has an indirect impact because immigrants have children. Immigrants are typically quite young when they arrive and they account for an increasing proportion of women of child-bearing age in the UK population (Table 1.2). Women who were born abroad also tend to have larger families than native women. Age-specific birth rates amongst immigrants have fallen considerably in recent years, but are still higher than amongst natives. These factors help to explain why the overall UK birth rate has increased in recent years. Official population projections take into account the

Table 1.2: Total fertility rates and population of UK-born and non UK-born women in 2007 and 2011

	2007			2007		
	UK-born	Non-UK born	Total pop.	UK-born	Non-UK born	Total pop.
Total fertility rate (number of children per woman)	1.80	2.51	1.91	1.89	2.28	1.96
Population of women aged 15–44 (millions)	10.68	1.81	12.48	10.17	2.23	12.40

impact of migration on the age structure but not its effect on age-specific fertility rates. These projections may therefore underestimate the impact of migration on future population growth, although by how much is uncertain.

Education and employment

Immigrants are on average better educated than the UK-born population. The difference is most marked amongst recent immigrants, of whom 57% have completed some form of higher education and only 6% finished school before they were 17 years of age (Table 1.3).

Table 1.3: Education and immigrant status (working-age population), 2014

Age finished Education	Percentage of group with each level of education UK-born	All immigrants	New immigrants
16 or under	46.1%	18.9%	6.2%
17-20	31.2%	37.3%	36.5%
21+	22.6%	43.8%	57.4%

The high level of education amongst immigrants is reflected in their occupations: 32% of those in work are employed in a managerial or higher professional occupation.[10] The corresponding share amongst the UK-born population is 29% (Wadsworth, 2015). Immigrants are also over-represented at the other end of the scale. Some 50% of immigrants from the A8 countries are employed in processing or elementary operations as compared to 16% of the UK-born population.

Employment rates vary widely amongst the immigrant population. In October-December 2013 the proportion of the UK-born population of working age with a job was 72.7%. For immigrants as a whole the figure was 69.3%.

Employment rates for immigrants from particular countries were as follows: Australia and New Zealand 85.9%, South Africa 82.5%, EU 77.9%, India 72.0%, Africa (excluding South Africa) 54.7%, Pakistan and Bangladesh 48.9%.[11]

2

Labour market impacts

Immigration has many economic benefits. Entrepreneurial or highly educated migrants bring valuable skills and help to establish economic links with their countries of origin. Many immigrants have a strong work ethic and have high aspirations for their children. New immigrants may also be more mobile than the local population and more willing to move into areas or occupations where there is a scarcity of some particular type of labour. In the case of the UK, this is especially true of recent migrants from central and eastern Europe, who are mostly young, without dependants and highly mobile when they first arrive. Borjas (2001) has called this 'greasing the wheels of industry'.

The main labour market variables affected by migration are wages, employment, unemployment, and labour force participation. The sign, magnitude and duration of these effects depend on a wide variety of factors and no simple generalisation is possible. Most econometric studies find that immigration has at most a small impact on the average worker, although certain particular types of worker may be quite seriously affected. However, most of the existing evidence on migration refers to an era of underlying dynamism when it was easier to absorb immigrants without significant harm to native workers. It may be of limited relevance to the recent past of prolonged recession and slow economic growth.

Theory

The conventional starting point for analysing the labour market impact of immigration is the following simple model. Labour is of uniform quality. All workers are identical from a productive point of view. They are all equally skilled and industrious and they all receive the same wage. There is no difference between foreign and native workers. Wages are flexible and rise or fall so as to clear the labour market.

In this model, immigration augments the supply of labour thereby intensifying competition for existing jobs. As a result wages fall. This leads firms to take on more labour so that both immigrants and natives are able to find work, although at a lower wage than before. However, this situation is only temporary. Lower wages mean higher profits. Firms will react to higher profits by investing in new productive capacity thereby increasing the demand for labour and reversing the initial fall in wages. After a time wages will return to their old level prior to immigration.

The above argument assumes that native wages are flexible and that firms are indifferent between migrants and natives. In practice, neither of these conditions may hold. Native workers may refuse to accept wage cuts as the price of keeping their jobs. Or firms may prefer migrants because they are better workers or easier to sack than natives. Either way, migrants may be employed in preference to natives. Alternatively, local regulations may prevent such 'exploitation' and ensure that migrants enjoy the same wages, conditions and security as natives. Even then, on a purely random basis, migrants will get some of the jobs that would otherwise have gone to natives. In all of these examples, immigration will initially cause native employment to fall and the result will be a surplus of labour in the local labour market. What happens over the longer run depends on the behaviour of investment. In a buoyant economy firms will respond to a surplus of labour by installing new capacity and creating new jobs for natives. Any job loss for native workers due to immigration will therefore be transitory.

In the above analysis, the immediate effect of immigration is to reduce either wages or employment for native workers. Over the longer run, in a buoyant economy, these losses will eventually be reversed, because immigration will stimulate more investment and faster economic growth. How rapidly this will occur in practice is an empirical question that I discuss below.

Complements and substitutes

The above analysis assumes that migrants and natives have similar skills and can be easily substituted for each other. However, this is not always the case. It may be that immigrants have characteristics that complement those of certain natives and their entry may enhance the productivity of the latter. For example, the labour of highly skilled immigrants may increase the productivity of low skilled native workers and increase the wages they command. Likewise, the activities of immigrant entrepreneurs may create employment for native workers. As a broad generalisation, native workers gain from the inflow of workers whose characteristics complement their own, but lose from the inflow of workers who are like themselves and against whom they must compete. The net effect of immigration on any particular category of native worker depends on the balance between these two effects. If the immigrants are mainly employed in skilled occupations then immigration is likely to benefit less skilled natives. If the immigrants enter low skill occupations, their entry will benefit skilled natives who enjoy cheaper goods and services, but it may also harm the low skilled natives they compete with. Note that there is a subtlety here. What matters are not simply the skills of the immigrants but also the types of job they get. Recent immigrants from eastern Europe are on average highly educated, but many of them work in low paid jobs where they compete with less skilled native workers. This is a waste of talent and there is an additional loss to GDP and the exchequer if they displace unskilled native workers.

Doing the jobs that native workers will not do

In rich countries many dirty, hard or low status jobs are increasingly occupied by migrants from poorer countries. These are said to be doing the jobs that native workers will not do. In practice this often means that suitable native workers will not do these jobs at the wages and conditions that employers are willing to offer. There are few jobs that natives will not do if conditions are reasonable and wages are sufficiently high. This is evident from a country like Finland which has few immigrants and yet seems to function rather well. Moreover, one of the reasons that jobs are low status and unattractive to natives is precisely because pay is low or they are increasingly dominated by migrant labour.

The 'lump of labour fallacy'

Claims that immigration harms native workers are sometimes based on the assumption that the total demand for labour is fixed, in which case each job taken by an immigrant means one less job for a native. This assumption is known as the 'lump of labour fallacy'. Stated in this extreme form it is, indeed, a fallacy. Immigration normally leads to faster economic growth and generates extra demand for labour. In this sense, immigrants bring extra jobs with them. However, the extra jobs may not appear immediately and there may be quite a long transition period during which native workers experience unemployment (or lower wages). Moreover, if there is a continuing inflow of migrants, the labour market may be in constant disequilibrium, with economic growth and new job creation lagging constantly behind the growth in labour supply due to immigration. In its extreme form the 'lump of labour fallacy' may well be a fallacy, but it points to a genuine issue.

Evidence

In the realm of theory economists mostly agree about the effects of immigration on native workers. There is less agreement about the scale and duration of these effects. This section begins by examining the international evidence and then goes on to focus explicitly on the UK.

International evidence

In a meta-analysis Longhi *et al* (2008) collated the results of 45 empirical studies on the labour market impacts of immigration published between 1982 and 2007. On average most of these effects were fairly small but there was a wide dispersion of results, reflecting different methodologies and different circumstances. The largest detrimental effects were reported for labour force participation. There was quite strong evidence that immigration discourages workless natives from entering or remaining in the labour market. The authors speculate that 'large adjustments in labour force participation might explain the apparently small adjustments in wages and/or (un)employment in response to immigration'.[1] They also report that immigration has a bigger negative effect on wages in the US than in Europe, whereas the negative effect on employment is greater in Europe. They speculate that this difference reflects institutional differences in the two areas. Wages are less flexible in Europe so that competition from immigrants is more likely to result in job losses for natives than lower wages. This observation is supported by the findings of Glitz (2012) who examines the impact of immigration of ethnic Germans into West Germany after the fall of the Berlin Wall. He estimates that 31 local workers were displaced for every 100 immigrants. Because of the highly regulated nature of the labour market at the time there was no discernible impact on relative wages. The reverse is likely to be the case in the US where wages are more flexible.

The effect of immigration on native workers has been most intensively studied in the US. One highly influential study by Borjas and Katz (1997) estimated that immigration explained 27% to 55% of the substantial decline in the relative wages of high school dropouts in the US over the period 1980-95.[2] Other papers by Borjas reach a similar conclusion (e.g. Borjas, 2013). In contrast, Ottoviani and Peri (2012) find that immigration has only a small impact on the wages of this group. Using a different methodology, Card (2001) finds that in some of America's gateway cities, such as Los Angeles, large-scale immigration during the period 1985-90 'significantly reduced employment rates for younger and less educated native workers'.[3] Elsewhere, Card (2005) and also Smith and Edmonston (1997) find that immigration has a surprisingly small impact on native workers of any variety.

Most studies in this area are concerned with individual countries. There are two important studies which take an international perspective. In their econometric study of EU countries, Angrist and Kugler (2003) find a pattern of 'reasonably stable negative effects' of immigration on native male employment.[4] The estimated effects vary according to the method of estimation, but in some cases they are large and statistically significant: up to 83 native male jobs lost for each 100 male immigrants. For women the results are mixed and more difficult to interpret.

> In a study of 18 OECD countries, including the UK, Jean and Jiménez (2007) conclude that their estimates do not find any permanent effect of immigration, measured as the share of immigrants in the labour force, upon natives' unemployment... however, the transitory impact may be substantial; its magnitude and duration largely depends on the persistence of unemployment shocks, and it may last between five and ten years.[5]

Five to 10 years is a long time and it refers to a one-off rise in the share of immigrants in the national labour force. The share of immigrants in all advanced OECD countries is on an upward trend and may continue rising for some years. If the estimates of Jean and Jiménez are correct, they imply that there will be a prolonged rise in native unemployment in some of these countries because of immigration.

Figure 2.1: Cumulative changes in employment since 1997 (thousands)

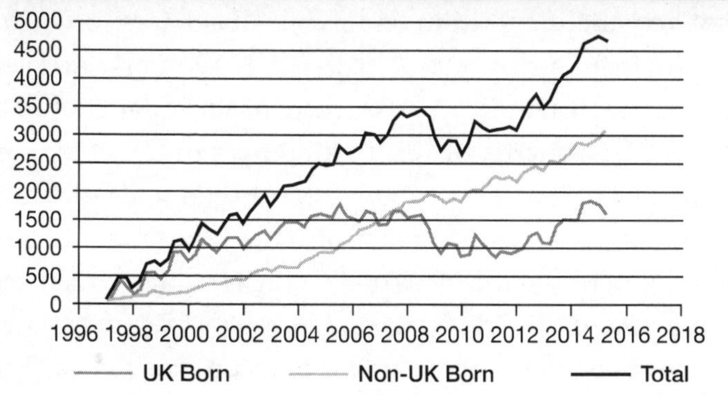

Figure 2.2: Employment rate UK-born age 16–64 (%)

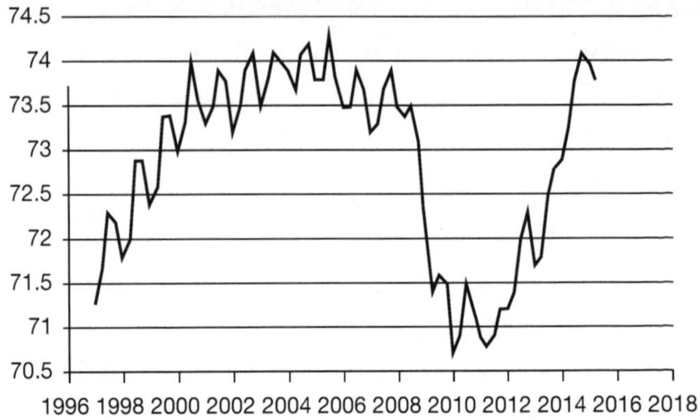

The UK has a relatively flexible labour market, so the employment effects supposedly identified by these authors should be smaller and less durable than those of the typical OECD economy. Even so, they could still be quite large.

This is an area of great uncertainty, so neither of the two international studies should be taken as infallible. However, they put a question mark over the optimistic claim that natives have little to fear from immigration.

Evidence from the UK: employment and unemployment

A casual examination of aggregate statistics would suggest that competition from migrants has damaged the employment prospects of native UK workers, at least during the economic crisis. Between the first quarter of 2008 and the first quarter of 2010, the number of UK natives in employment fell by over 700,000 or 3% (Figure 2.1). During the same period, the number of foreign-born workers in employment remained virtually constant. Since then the employment of UK natives has recovered and their employment rate is now similar to its previous peak. The behaviour of employment during the crisis does not prove definitively that migrants displaced native workers but it does suggest there is a case to answer.

Reliable evidence on this topic is hard to come by. Dustmann *et al* (2003) use census data to analyse the impact of immigration on unemployment. They estimate that a one percentage point increase in the proportion of immigrants in a local population will raise the unemployment rate by 0.23 to 0.6 percentage points.[6] This may overstate the impact on natives, since the additional unemployment includes immigrants. Using a different data source the same study finds smaller and less statistically significant effects. A number of studies by these and other authors find that the impact of immigration on native UK employment or unemployment is either small or statistically insignificant.[7] The latest of these is by Lucchino *et al* (2012), which examines the impact of migration inflows on the claimant count unemployment rate. They find no association between migrant inflows and claimant unemployment. They also test for whether the impact of migration on claimant unemployment varies according to the state of the economic cycle. They find no evidence of a more adverse impact during periods of low growth or recent recession.

One exception is Nathan (2011) who finds a negative and statistically significant relationship between migrant shares and native employment rates, with the impacts strongest amongst the intermediate and low skilled.[8]

An analysis by the UK Migration Advisory Committee (MAC, 2012) also finds that immigration has adversely affected native employment. The authors of this report 'estimate that an increase of 100 foreign-born working-age migrants in the UK was associated with a reduction of 23 natives in employment for the period 1995 to 2010'. Using the 'output gap' as an indicator of the demand for labour, they estimate that an inflow of 100 foreign-born working-age migrants is associated with a reduction in native employment of approximately 30 in the same year when the output gap is zero or negative.[10] The estimated association is statistically insignificant when the output gap is positive. The authors comment that these results seem 'sensible, since migrants are more likely to compete with natives for jobs during an economic downturn when native unemployment is high and job vacancies are low.'[11]

The authors of the MAC report also examine whether immigration from the EU has had a different impact from other types of immigration. Their estimated coefficients for the two types of migration are very similar in magnitude and sign, but of different statistical significance: the non-EU coefficient is significant, but the EU coefficient is not. These findings are summarised in the text as follows:

> Our results suggest that a one-off increase of 100 in the inflow of working-age non-EU born migrants is associated with a reduction in native employment of 23 over the period 1995 to 2010. Our results indicate that inflows of working-age EU migrants did not have a statistically significant association with native employment.[12]

Whilst strictly correct, this summary fails to mention that the estimated coefficients on EU and non-EU migration are in fact very similar. The casual reader might interpret this summary to mean that non-EU migration and EU migration have in reality had radically different effects. This is rather implausible as the authors themselves concede elsewhere in the report. In an appendix discussing their results in detail they state that they 'cannot reject the possibility that the association between non-EU migrants and native employment rates was the same as that for EU migrants'.[13]

The MAC analysis has been extended in a recent Home Office report (Devlin *et al*, 2014). The report argues that studies which focus on unemployment are likely to underestimate the impact of immigration on native employment. If migration into an area reduces job opportunities for natives, they may become discouraged and stop looking for work. Such people will be classified as economically inactive and will not be included in the unemployment statistics. To explore this issue, Devlin *et al* repeat the MAC regression analysis using unemployment instead of employment as the dependent variable. The effect is dramatic. There is a clear negative association between native employment and immigration, but virtually no statistical association between native unemployment and immigration. This would suggest that many of the natives who are directly or indirectly displaced by immigration drop out of the labour force and are no longer classified as unemployed. Studies which rely on visible unemployment to estimate the impact of immigration on natives, such as Lucchino *et al* (2012), will miss this discouraged worker effect. They will therefore underestimate the impact of immigration on native employment.

Devlin *et al* also repeat the MAC analysis for other time periods. The results provide some support for the MAC suggestion that immigration had more impact on native employment during the recession than during the preceding boom. The MAC analysis ends in 2010. When this is extended to 2012, the estimates are virtually unchanged. As before, the coefficients for EU and non-EU migrants are virtually identical, although the former is not statistically significant. As before, the findings are consistent with the hypothesis that EU and non-EU migration had identical effects, at least during the recession.[14]

The bulk of the Home Office report is devoted to a survey of the evidence on labour displacement in the UK. Their conclusions are summarised as follows:

- 'Overall, our assessment is that there is relatively little evidence that migration has caused statistically significant displacement of UK natives from the labour market in periods when the economy has been strong. However, in line with some recent studies, there is evidence for some labour market displacement in recent years when the economy was in recession'.
- 'Displacement effects are also more likely to be identified in periods when net migration volumes are high, rather than when volumes are low – so analyses that focus on data prior to the 2000s are less likely to find any impacts. In addition, where displacement effects are observed, these tend to be concentrated on low skilled natives'.
- 'This suggests that the labour market adjusts to increased net migration when economic conditions are good. But during a recession, and when net migration volumes are high as in recent years, it appears that the labour market adjusts at a slower rate and some short-term impacts are observed'.
- 'To date there has been little evidence in the literature of a statistically significant impact from EU migration on native employment outcomes, although significant EU migration is still a relatively recent phenomenon and this does not imply that impacts do not occur in some circumstances'.
- 'The evidence also suggests that where there has been a displacement effect from a particular cohort of migrants, this dissipates over time – that is, any displacement impacts from one set of new arrivals gradually decline as the labour market adjusts, as predicted by economic theory'.[15]

This is a fair, if somewhat cautious, summary of the evidence on labour displacement. In particular, it correctly points out that much of the evidence is of limited value because it relates to a period when the demand for labour was strong and there were relatively few immigrants competing with natives for jobs. Under such conditions, the amount of labour displacement is likely to be small and hard to identify using available evidence.

My one quibble concerns EU migration. The Home Office summary states that there is little evidence in the literature of a statistically significant impact from EU migration on native employment. This is technically correct, but as explained above in the context of the MAC report, this does not mean that in reality EU migration has had little impact. It simply means that there is too much noise in the system and too many confounding factors to permit reliable estimation of the EU impact. It would be equally consistent with statistical evidence to conclude that EU and non-EU immigration had similar effects. Indeed, this is the most plausible interpretation.

Evidence from the UK: wages

There have been a number of studies seeking to quantify the effect of immigration on wages in the UK. Taken as a whole, these studies suggest that immigration has had little effect on average wages, but has had a significant effect on the wages of certain types of worker.[16]

Nickell and Saleheen (2008) examine the impact of immigration on the wages of various occupational groups. They find a reduction for skilled production workers and a much larger reduction for semi/unskilled service workers. In the latter case, they estimate the reduction to be in the realm of 5%. Manacorda *et al* (2007) also find that unskilled immigration harms the local unskilled workforce, but its effects are confined mainly to previous immigrants. This is because later immigrants enter the same unskilled occupations as their predecessors, with whom they compete. Using data for Wales, Lemos (2010) finds little or no impact of immigration on the bottom half of the wage distribution and some positive impact on the wages of more highly paid workers. Nathan (2011) finds no statistically significant impact on any skill group.

Dustmann *et al* (2008) examine the impact of immigration across the whole spectrum of income distribution. They find that immigration has led to a small reduction in the wages of the bottom 20% of earners. The modest size in this reduction is not surprising since the study is concerned with the combined effect of all types of immigration. Economic theory suggests that different types of immigration affect different types of worker in different ways. Many of the migrants into the UK have gone into skilled occupations where their entry may have helped to create jobs and higher wages for local unskilled workers. However, many immigrants have also gone into unskilled occupations where they compete with unskilled locals, thereby reducing employment opportunities and wages for the latter. Thus, local unskilled workers have gained from some types of immigration and lost from others. It is not surprising that the overall impact of immigration on unskilled workers has been small.

Dustmann *et al* (2008) also find that the average worker has experienced a modest gain from immigration. They estimate that an increase of one percentage point in the foreign-born share of the working-age population leads to an increase of between 0.2% and 0.3% in average wages. Between 1997 and 2008 the foreign-born share of the working-age population rose by 5.3 percentage points (from 8.6% to 13.9%). If Dustmann *et al* are correct this would imply a total increase of between 1.1% and 1.6% in the average wage due to immigration over the period in question.[17]

This finding has certain features that deserve mention. If immigration were to stop, the gains from past immigration would gradually disappear. To maintain the 1.1%–1.6% increase in the average wage already achieved requires substantial immigration in the future. To achieve a further increase of the same amount in real wages would require raising the share of foreign-born in the working-age population from 13.9% to 19.2%. This would require a permanently high rate of immigration and the result would be rapid and indefinite population growth. Unrestrained population growth would eventually have a negative impact on the standard of living through its environmental effects such as overcrowding, congestion and loss of amenity. Such losses would ultimately outweigh the small gain in average wages apparently resulting from mass immigration. This is the subject of the next chapter.

Conclusion

At one time most economists claimed that immigration had a negligible effect on the employment of natives. This consensus has begun to fray in recent years as new evidence has emerged. An econometric analysis by the official Migration Advisory Committee strongly suggests that immigration damages the job prospects of lower skilled natives when the labour market is slack. There is evidence from other sources that immigration may also have a transitory effect on native employment even in boom times. In addition, there is evidence that competition from immigrants may result in lower wages for low skilled local workers, including previous immigrants. The liberal media are quick to denounce as xenophobia the claim that immigrants take jobs from local workers and push down their wages. This claim may be exaggerated, but it is not always false.

3

Population growth and ageing

As birth rates fall and life expectancy increases the world is getting older. This process is most advanced in economically more developed countries, but it is happening even in many poorer countries. UN demographers have made long-range projections of what the future size and age structure of national populations would be in the absence of international migration. These projections indicate that the natural speed of ageing in the UK is about average for a developed country. It is somewhat faster than in the US but slower than in Germany and southern Europe and much slower than in Korea and Japan. Concern about ageing and the resulting burden on the economically active population is often used as a justification for supporting large-scale immigration. The aim is to rejuvenate the population by importing large numbers of young workers to boost the active labour force and generate the taxes required to support the rising number of pensioners. An alternative or parallel policy is to lift the retirement age, thereby simultaneously increasing the size of the working population and reducing the number of retirees.

One potential downside to large-scale immigration is its impact on population size. In a country concerned about population decline, such as Germany, the extra population resulting from immigration may be regarded as a benefit. This does not apply to the UK, where population decline is not an immediate prospect and many people consider the country to be already overcrowded.

Such demographic issues are the subject of this chapter. The chapter documents how immigration can help to rejuvenate the UK population, but only at the cost of faster population growth. To the extent that fast population growth is seen as undesirable, the resulting costs must be weighed against the presumed benefits of rejuvenation through immigration. It may be better to settle for less immigration and much slower population growth at the cost of somewhat faster ageing.

Population and age structure

Migration affects both the size and age structure of the resident population. It also affects many other features of the country such as ethnic and religious composition and voting patterns.

Immigration adds to the population both directly through the influx of additional people and indirectly through its impact on the number of children born in the receiving country: immigrants have children, and their children have children, and so on. Emigration has the opposite effect. Projections by the Office for National Statistics (ONS) imply that for each 1 million immigrants who arrive in the UK, there will be an eventual addition to population equal to 1.5 million.[1] The latter figure may be an underestimate because it ignores the fact that on average immigrants have more children than the local UK population.[2] However, this differential may narrow or even be eliminated in the future as fertility rates fall in the migrants' countries of origin. Moreover, a larger fraction of migrants now come from low-fertility EU countries.

When interpreting migration statistics it is important to distinguish between net and gross migration. Immigrants have a different age-profile from emigrants. This in itself has demographic implications even when the numbers of immigrants and emigrants are equal. For example, suppose that a thousand older natives leave the country and are replaced by a thousand immigrants of child-bearing age. Since inflows and outflows are numerically equal, this will be recorded as zero net migration in the aggregate statistics. However, it will have an effect on the age structure of the population, and hence on the national birth rate. Being mostly young, the immigrants will have more child-bearing years ahead of them than the older emigrants whom they replace. If age-specific fertility rates are the same for both groups, the net impact on the overall birth rate will be positive. The reduction in births due to emigration will be outweighed by the additional births due to immigration. This is a pure age-effect which holds even if immigration and emigration are numerically equal. This effect will be reinforced if the immigrants come from high fertility cultures.

Projections

Table 3.1 compares various projections the ONS has made for the UK population and age structure over the period 2012-2087. It also incudes a projection which is derived by extrapolation from the ONS projections.[3] The same information is illustrated graphically in more detail in Figures 3.1 and 3.2. These projections should be treated with caution. They are only as good as the assumptions they make and become progressively less reliable as the time horizon is extended. However, the differences between projections due to migration are likely to be fairly accurate over quite a long time horizon since they are determined mainly by their assumed migration flows.

Table 3.1: Projected changes in UK population and age structure

Projection	Annual net migration	Population (millions)				Change 2012-2087
		2012	2037	2062	2087	
ONS natural change	0	63.7	67.5	66.3	63.8	+0.0
Very low migration (est.)	50,000	63.7	70.1	72.3	74.2	+10.5
ONS low migration	105,000	63.7	71.6	76.0	80.1	+16.4
ONS principal projection	165,000	63.7	73.3	79.9	86.5	+22.8
ONS high migration	225,000	63.7	75.0	83.9	92.9	+29.2

Projection	Annual net migration	Dependency ratio (number age 65+ per 100 age 16-64				Change 2012-2087
		2012	2037	2062	2087	
ONS natural change	0	26.5	46.2	56.3	61.2	+34.7
Very low migration (est.)	50,000	26.5	44.0	50.1	54.0	+27.5
ONS low migration	105,000	26.5	42.9	48.5	52.7	+26.2
ONS principal projection	165,000	26.5	41.9	46.9	51.5	+25.0
ONS high migration	225,000	26.5	40.8	45.6	50.5	+24.0

Source: ONS except for the very low migration projection which is derived by extrapolation from the ONS projections. The natural change projection assumes there is no migration at all.

All projections make identical assumptions about age-specific birth and death rates. They differ only in their assumptions about migration. The principal projection is based on assumptions that the ONS statisticians consider to

Figure 3.1: UK population projections 2012–2087 (millions)

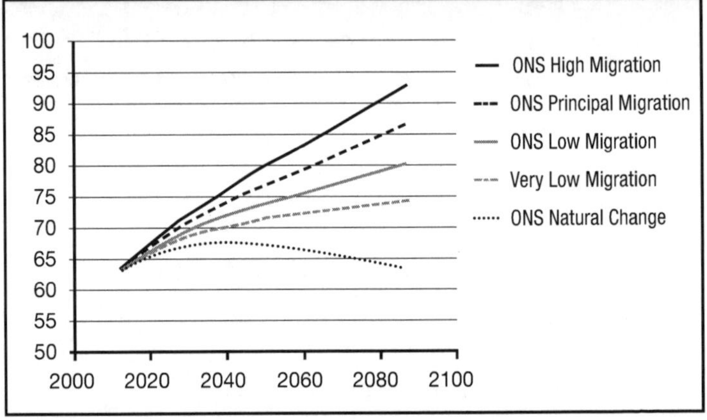

Figure 3.2: Dependency ratio (65+/16–54) 2012–2087 (%)

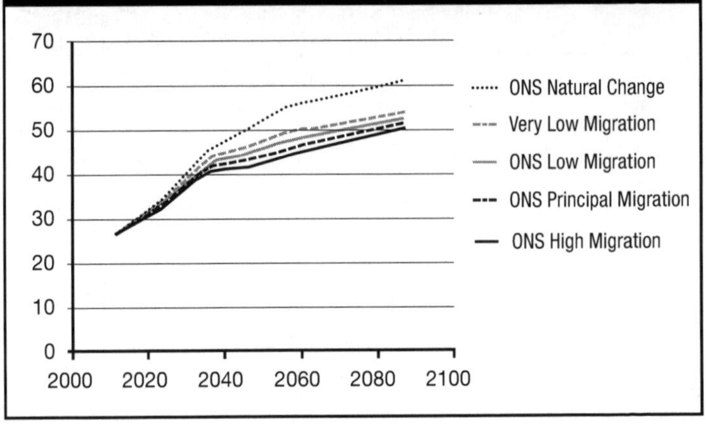

be most plausible. It is their best guess as to how future population will evolve. The projection labelled 'natural change' assumes that no one at all enters or leaves the country. Thus, all future changes in the size and age structure of the population are the result of births and deaths amongst the initial population and their descendants. The remaining projections assume progressively higher rates of net migration. The age structure of the population is summarised by the dependency ratio. This ratio is the number of persons aged 65+ per hundred persons aged 16-64. The main points to note are as follows:

- Under all projections, the population gets older through the course of time and the dependency ratio increases rapidly, especially in the earlier years. Migration helps to retard the speed of ageing but does not prevent it.
- With no migration at all (natural change variant) the UK population rises by a modest amount for the first few decades and then starts to fall. By 2087, the population is virtually the same as at the beginning.
- The increase of population under some of the projections is very large. Under the ONS high migration projection (net migration 225,000 p.a.), population increases by 29.2 million over the period. This is equivalent to adding a city almost the size of Birmingham to the UK population every two-and-a-half years for the next 75 years. Note that the assumed rate of net migration under this projection is less than the average of 236,000 p.a. for UK net migration during the period 2001-2014 and is well below the latest figure of 330,000 for the year ending March 2015.
- Increasing the rate of net migration has only a modest effect on the dependency ratio but a relatively large impact on population growth. This can be seen by comparing the very low migration and high migration projections. These differ only in their assumed migration rate. With very low net migration (50,000 p.a.) the dependency ratio rises to 54.0% in 2087 and population to 74.2 million. With high migration (225,000 p.a.), the corresponding numbers are 50.5% and 92.9 million.

Comparing these two scenarios, the extra migration required to reduce the dependency ratio by 3.5 percentage points adds an extra 18.7 million to national population by 2087. This works out at 5.3 million extra people for each one percentage point reduction in the dependency ratio.

- The effects of migration on the age structure are mostly front-loaded. Higher rates of net immigration reduce the dependency ratio during the initial decades, but from then onwards the gaps between the projections remain fairly constant. This is because the young immigrants who enter the UK during the initial years eventually reach old age and new immigrants are then required simply to preserve the age structure. Rejuvenation through immigration is an endless treadmill. To maintain a once and for all reduction in the dependency ratio requires a never ending stream of immigrants. Once the inflow stops, the age structure will revert to its original trajectory.

The above examples illustrate how migration involves a trade-off between rejuvenation and population growth. Immigration on the scale envisaged under the ONS high migration scenario would slow down the ageing of the UK population somewhat, but it would also involve a much faster growth in population. Some people would be perfectly happy with this outcome. Many others would not. To the extent that fast population growth is seen as undesirable, the resulting costs must be weighed against the benefits of rejuvenation through immigration. Many people would consider it better to settle for much less immigration and much slower population growth at the cost of slightly faster ageing. This outcome is illustrated in the very low migration projection. The choice is ultimately a matter of personal preference.

One method of responding to population ageing is to lift the state pension age, thereby encouraging people to retire later. This increases the number of people of working age and reduces the number of pensioners. Such changes are already underway in the UK. Using this alternative measure of age structure, the trade-off between rejuvenation and population growth is even more unfavourable than before. Under the very low migration scenario the ratio of pensioners to working age population rises to 45.4% in 2087. Under the high migration scenario the terminal value of this ratio is 42.3%. The immigration required to achieve this small reduction adds an extra 18.7 million to the national population by 2087 over and above the increase of 10.5 million that occurs under the very low migration scenario.

Consequences

Population growth has a number of potential advantages. Provided most of the immigrants gain well-paid jobs without displacing existing workers, they will generate a fiscal surplus which can be used to finance government expenditure on public goods. For example, with a larger employed population a given military establishment can be supported at a lower per capita cost. The same applies to the national debt. Of course, none of these benefits will be forthcoming if the immigrants fail to get work or if they earn so little that they absorb more in government expenditure than they pay in taxes. In this case they will be a burden on the exchequer. The fiscal aspects of migration are discussed in chapter 4. A larger population also means a larger and denser home market for home-produced goods and services, allowing suppliers to achieve local and national economies of scale. This is of less importance to the UK than it used to be since a greater proportion of goods and services are now exported and many firms rely less on the home market than formerly. A larger population implies a greater density of population and hence the more intensive use of otherwise underutilised collective facilities. This may be a significant advantage in a region of the country with a low population density.

There are also dynamic economies of scale to consider. Nicholas Kaldor (1966) famously argued that UK manufacturing was being held back by a shortage of labour. If there were more labour, he argued, the output of the manufacturing sector would grow faster and this would stimulate productivity growth. This claim was hotly disputed at the time, but is no longer relevant in the UK of today. Nobody seriously argues that UK manufacturing is currently being held back by an absolute shortage of labour. There is plenty of unskilled labour available. What is often lacking are workers with the right skills. This is not a problem to be solved simply by increasing the size of the labour force through immigration.

Under the projections considered in this chapter, migration causes the population of working age to grow slightly faster than the total population. Other things being equal, this means that future per capita income is slightly larger because of migration. For example, people of working age are 58.4% of the total population in 2087 under the high migration scenario and 56.8% under the very low migration scenario. Provided employment rates and labour productivity were the same under the two scenarios, GDP per capita would be 3% higher in 2087 with high migration than with very low migration. However, there are important provisos. What happens to the employment rates and productivity of immigrants will depend on their human capacities and how successfully they are integrated into the UK labour market.

Population growth has implications for the volume of national production and hence for the international standing of the UK in Europe. UK population is currently growing rapidly, and under any realistic scenario it will continue growing throughout this century. In contrast, the German population is falling and is projected by UN demographers to continue falling. If these trends persist, the UK will eventually have a larger population than Germany and by implication a larger economy. Under the ONS high migration scenario, the UK would overtake Germany in about 30 years, and under the very low migration scenario it would require about 40 years for this to happen.[4]

There are also disadvantages to consider. Population growth may lead to housing shortage and pressure on public facilities such as schools, hospitals and the transport infrastructure. Such problems can in principle be handled by building more homes, enlarging existing schools and hospitals or building new ones, widening existing roads or building new ones, and increasing the capacity of the rail network and airports. This would not be a once-and-for-all investment programme. Sustained population growth would require an ever increasing number of homes, hospitals, schools and transport facilities. Ideally, the required investment should be planned in advance so that extra facilities become available at the time they are needed rather than after the event when problems have become too severe to ignore. But planning is not a panacea. However well planned, the changes required to accommodate a rapidly growing population may be both difficult and costly. Suitable land may not be available except at great material or environmental cost. Re-engineering existing cities to accommodate the additional population may be very costly, and expansion into the surrounding countryside may be resisted by local people. In the UK there is often strong opposition to building on the green belt around our cities, especially in the southern part of the country where the pressure on land is greatest. The present government has revealed plans to build two new garden cities to relieve the housing shortage in the south-east. With immigration at the rate envisaged under the ONS high migration scenario, a new town the size of Letchworth Garden City would have to be built every month for the next 75 years simply to keep up with the growth of population. This takes no account of the additional homes required to eliminate the existing housing shortage.

Many of our railway lines and major roads are already overcrowded, especially in the more populous parts of the country. The 10 most overcrowded peak rail services in England in autumn 2012 were between 49% and 65% over their maximum allowable standard class passenger capacity limit.[5] They were all London routes. Since the economy started to pick up, the proportion of on-time journeys on motorways and A roads has fallen and is now only 77%.[6] It would be a massive and controversial undertaking to increase transport capacity in line with the demand growth implied by continued large-scale immigration.

There is also water to consider. The most water-stressed regions of England and Wales are mostly located in the east and south-east of England, which are on a par with southern Spain and Italy. However, a report by the Environment Agency (2008) has warned that

> there are considerable pressures on water resources throughout England and Wales... there are many catchments where there is no water available for abstraction at low flows. In addition, some catchments are over licensed or over-abstracted, and we need to restore a sustainable abstraction regime.[7]

Population growth is identified in this report as a major source of future strain on water resources. The negative consequences of population growth are most severe in London and the south-east. These areas are currently magnets because of their high demand for labour. How long this will continue to be the case is hard to predict. In the late 1970s, people were bemoaning the decline of the London economy because it was losing manufacturing jobs, yet within 20 years it was experiencing a spectacular boom in financial and other services. Who knows how things will look in 20 or 30 years' time? London's financial sector is not currently on the brink of collapse and its long-term future may be less rosy than used to be thought. Foreign competition, tougher regulations and the rise of new competitors may herald a period of slow growth for the City of London, with knock-on effects on the wider regional economy. It could be that the locus of economic dynamism will shift away from the south and east towards other parts of the UK where population pressure is less severe. Only time will tell.

Conclusion

The message of this chapter is simple. Immigration helps to slow down the inevitable ageing of the UK population and also leads to faster population growth. To the extent that fast population growth is seen as undesirable, the resulting costs must be weighed against the presumed benefits of rejuvenation through immigration. It may be better to settle for less immigration and much slower population growth at the cost of somewhat faster ageing. A rate of net migration equal to 50,000 annually is almost as effective at rejuvenating the national population as a much higher rate of net migration. It does so with much less impact on population growth.

4

The fiscal impact of migration

There has been extensive debate in the media about the impact of migration on government finances. A belief that immigrants impose a significant burden on UK taxpayers has fuelled hostility towards large-scale immigration. Others have argued for a liberal policy towards immigration on the grounds that migrants, especially those of European origin, pay more in taxes than they receive in government expenditure. Given the intensity of public debate there is a surprising degree of consensus amongst experts about the fiscal impacts of immigration. Some types of immigrant pay more in taxes than is spent on them and their families by the government. For other types the reverse is the case. The overall impact of immigration on government finances depends on the precise mix of these types, but the aggregate fiscal effect is typically small as a percentage of GDP.

Methodology

To estimate the fiscal consequences of migration is not easy.[1] There are several basic methods available and there are many choices to be made concerning such issues as the treatment of public goods, and the classification of the locally-born children of immigrants. One issue largely ignored in the literature is that of employment displacement. Despite some evidence to the contrary it is conventionally assumed that immigration has no impact on the employment level of natives. There are two basic methods for assessing the fiscal implications of migration: 'static' and 'dynamic'. The static (cash-flow) method takes a snapshot of the economy at a particular moment in time, and estimates the amount of government revenue (taxes etc) generated by a particular group of migrants in a given year and also the amount they receive from the government in the form of cash benefits and public services. The dynamic method looks forward and examines the entire future stream of revenues and expenditures resulting from a given inflow of migrants. This takes into account the future life course of migrants and also what happens to their descendants. The dynamic method is superior from a theoretical point of view, but may be difficult to apply in practice.

No matter what approach is chosen, static or dynamic, certain decisions must be taken with regard to the allocation of government expenditure on goods and services. In some cases, such as education and health, the total cost of providing recipients with a given level of utility is roughly proportional to the number of recipients involved. For accounting purposes, such expenditures can be allocated on a simple pro rata basis. However, not all expenditure is of this type. For example, immigration may lead to conflict and congestion, and to preserve the status quo may require a disproportionate rise in expenditure on such items as policing and infrastructure. Conversely, the cost of providing a given level of service, such as defence, may be only loosely related to population size and at the margin may be unaffected by immigration. An army of 100,000 may be able to defend a country of 70 million just as well as a country of 60 million. Items whose cost is independent of population size are known as 'pure public goods'. In the case of pure public goods, an increase in the labour force due to immigration has the beneficial effect of allowing fixed costs to be spread over a greater number of taxpayers.

Many studies on fiscal impact consider two kinds of scenario. There is what Dustmann and Frattini (2013a) call the 'average cost scenario'. This ascribes all government expenditure on goods and services to migrants on a pro rata basis in proportion to their share in the relevant population (share of children, share of adult population etc). In contrast, the 'marginal cost scenario' ascribes government expenditure on pure public goods, such as defence or central administration, entirely to natives. The rationale for this approach is that migrants should only be held accountable for the extra expenditure that is the result of immigration. Expenditure that would have occurred anyway in the absence of immigration should be ignored.

Comparing these two approaches, the marginal cost scenario gives a more accurate picture of how immigration affects government finances. It includes only the extra government expenditure that is due to immigration. Estimates derived under the average cost scenario have a different philosophical basis. They start from the notion that government expenditure on pure public goods, such as defence or central administration, is undertaken on behalf of the entire community. As members of this community it is only 'fair' that migrants should make a proportionate contribution to these expenditures. This principle of fairness should apply even to pure public goods whose scale and cost is unaffected by immigration. This principle derives from the idea of a national community to which the migrants now belong. As equal members of this community, they should pay their equal share.[2]

The distinction between these two approaches is illustrated by the following example. Two friends rent an apartment. They pay a fixed amount of £300 a week in rent which includes all running costs except for food. A stranger asks if he can move in with them and they agree. At the end of the week he pays them for the food he has consumed and also makes a contribution of £20 towards the rent. The friends say this is not fair and that the stranger should pay his equal share of the rent. They ask for an additional £80. The stranger argues that he has paid all of the extra costs due to his presence in the apartment plus an additional £20. The friends are therefore better off than if he had never moved in. Under marginal cost accounting, the stranger has a financial surplus equal to £20. This surplus indicates how much the others members of the group gain financially from the stranger's presence. Under average cost accounting, he has a deficit equal to £80. This deficit indicates how far the stranger's contribution falls short of his equal share.

International evidence

The fiscal impact of migration depends on the types of immigrant concerned and their insertion into the local economy. Highly educated, skilled or talented immigrants, provided they gain suitable employment, normally make a positive fiscal contribution. They pay more in taxes than they absorb in government expenditure. Such migrants come disproportionately, though not exclusively, from developed countries. Even unskilled immigrants may make a positive fiscal contribution provided they get jobs and do not displace local workers, and provided they and their families do not make large demands on the welfare state. At the opposite end of the spectrum are migrants who receive public support but do not pay tax because they are without gainful employment. Many asylum seekers or married women from developing countries are in this category. So, too, are the children and aged relatives of working migrants.

Table 4.1: OECD estimates of the net fiscal impact of immigrants under alternative assumptions, 2007-09 average (per cent of GDP)

	Baseline	Baseline plus per-capita allocation of public goods (except defence and debt interest)	Baseline plus per-capita allocation of public goods (except defence)
Austria	0.12	-0.37	-0.80
Belgium	0.76	0.06	-0.43
Czech Republic	-0.01	-0.28	-0.31
Denmark	0.11	-0.31	-0.39
Finland	0.16	-0.08	-0.13
France	-0.52	-0.52	-0.84
Germany	-1.13	-1.93	-2.32
Hungary	0.08	-0.11	-0.18
Ireland	-0.23	-1.23	-1.41
Italy	0.98	0.97	0.61
Luxembourg	2.02	0.37	0.24
Netherlands	0.40	-0.01	-0.14
Norway	0.42	0.60	0.49
Poland	-0.32	-0.42	-0.45
Portugal	0.52	0.27	0.13
Slovak Republic	-0.06	-0.16	-0.18
Spain	0.54	0.07	-0.05
Sweden	0.20	-0.37	-0.57
Switzerland	1.95	1.42	1.16
United Kingdom	0.46	-0.01	-0.26
United States	0.03	-0.64	-1.00
Average	0.30	-0.12	-0.31

In countries where there has been large-scale immigration over a long period of time, the stock of migrants and their descendants normally contains a wide spread of different types and age groups. This explains why estimates of the fiscal contribution of the immigrant population as a whole are typically quite small. The positive contribution of some migrants is largely or wholly offset by the negative contribution of others. This finding holds across a variety of countries and methodologies. In an extensive survey of the international evidence some years ago Rowthorn (2008) concluded that most estimates of the net fiscal contribution of immigration lie within the range ±1% of GDP. A more recent survey by the OECD (2013) supports this conclusion. The OECD's own estimates are summarized in Table 4.1.

The baseline estimates in Table 4.1 exclude expenditure on public goods, such as government administration, policing, defence and interest on the national debt. The remaining columns indicate how the results are affected if certain types of public good are included. The average fiscal impact of migration for the countries shown varies between -0.31% and +0.30% of GDP, depending on the list of included items. For the UK, the fiscal impact lies between -0.26% and +0.46% of GDP.

Evidence from the UK

The first systematic study of the fiscal impact of migration into the UK was done for the Home Office (Gott and Johnson, 2002). This study was later updated and slightly modified by the Institute for Public Policy Research (Sriskandarajah *et al*, 2005). The updated study estimated the net fiscal contribution of migrants to be -0.04% of GDP. Various potential adjustments to the IPPR estimate were considered by Rowthorn (2008). These adjustments included the re-allocation of defence expenditure, the re-classification of the children of mixed native/non-native parentage, and a budget balance condition. Depending on which adjustments were incorporated into the estimate, the net fiscal contribution of migrants was in the range ± 0.66% of GDP.

Dustmann and Frattini

The most detailed estimates of the fiscal impact of UK immigration are contained in a working paper by Dustmann and Frattini (2013a), henceforth D&F. This paper has received a great deal of media attention and is interesting in its own right, so it is worth a detailed examination. D&F distinguish between migrants born in countries of the European Economic Area (EEA)[3] and those born elsewhere. They also distinguish between migrants who arrived after 2000 and those who arrived previously.[4] Their main conclusion is that recent migrants from the EEA have generated, and continue to generate, a large fiscal surplus in relation to their numbers. The taxes they pay have consistently exceeded by a considerable margin the amount they receive from the government in the form of cash benefits and public services. Recent migrants from outside the EEA also generated a fiscal surplus over the period 2001-2011 as a whole. The picture is much less favourable for migrants who arrived before 2001.

D&F present two main types of estimate. The estimates labelled 'average cost scenario' assume that all government expenditure on public goods is allocated to migrants on a pro rata basis in proportion to their share in the relevant population (share of children, share of adult population etc). The estimates labelled 'marginal cost scenario' ascribe government expenditure on 'pure' public goods entirely to natives. In the D&F classification, 'pure' public goods include government administration, defence, interest on the national debt, and economic services such as transport.

Figure 4.1a shows D&F's estimates of the overall fiscal balance for all migrants calculated according to the two methods just described. Under the average cost scenario, for most of the time prior to the financial crisis this balance fluctuated between -£200 and -£800 per migrant in 2011 prices; following the crisis it deteriorated sharply to reach nearly -£2,000 in 2009. The picture is more favourable under the marginal cost scenario. Under this scenario, there is a surplus for most of the time, and the deficit following the crisis is relatively small.

It is instructive to examine recent and established migrants separately.[5] The fiscal balance of established (pre-2001) migrants is on a clear downward trend for most of the time (Figure 4.1b). Even under the favourable marginal cost scenario, this balance is in deficit from around 2002 onwards. The picture is much rosier for recent (post-2000) migrants. The fiscal balance for these migrants is almost always in surplus and improves slightly in the years leading up to the financial crisis (Figure 4.1c). There is a sharp deterioration following the crisis, but even under the worst case scenario their fiscal balance never shows a significant deficit.

For completeness, Figure 4.1d repeats the above exercise for UK natives. In this case, the fiscal trajectory for the average cost scenario lies above the trajectory for the marginal cost scenario. This is because a larger share of expenditure on public goods is ascribed to natives under

Figure 4.1a: Fiscal balance 1995–2011, all migrants (£ per capita, 2011 prices)

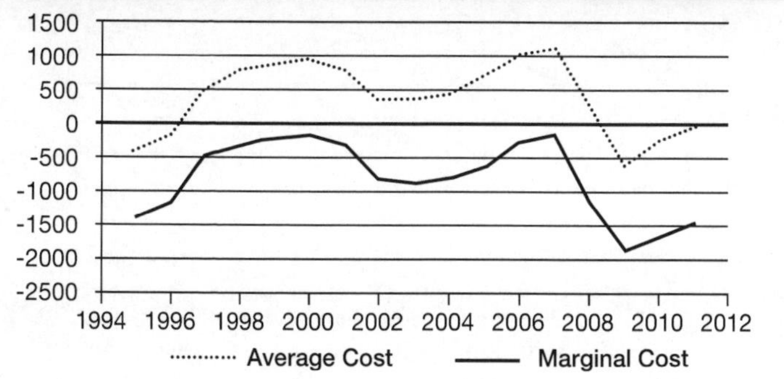

Figure 4.1b: Fiscal balance 1995–2011, pre-2001 migrants (£ per capita, 2011 prices)

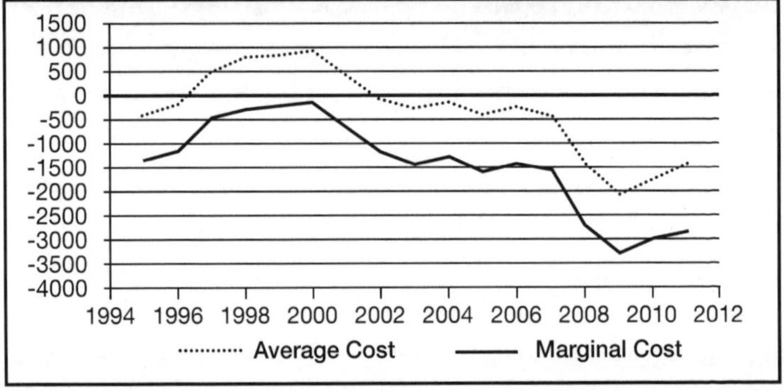

Figure 4.1c: Fiscal balance 1995–2011, post-2001 migrants (£ per capita, 2011 prices)

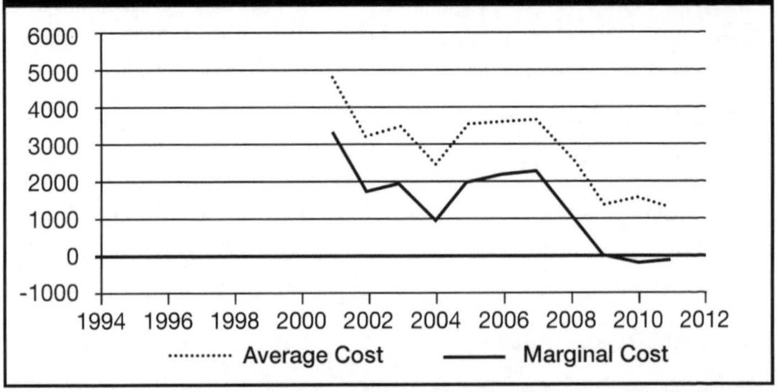

Figure 4.1d: Fiscal balance 1995–2011, UK natives (£ per capita, 2011 prices)

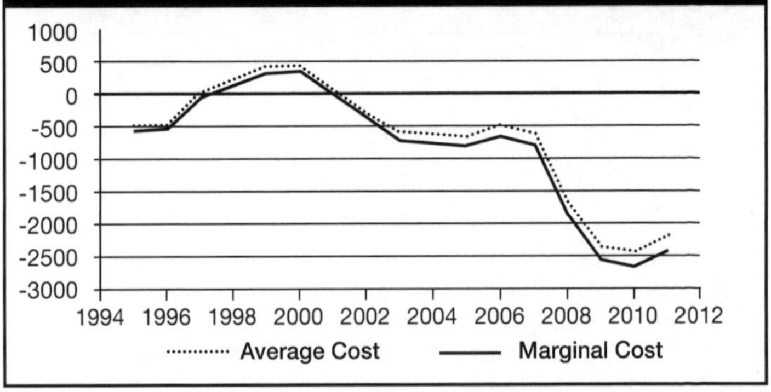

Table 4.2: Balance of revenue minus expenditure Total 2001–2011

Average cost scenario

	EEA	Non-EEA	Total
	£ billions (at 2011 prices)		
Pre-2001 migrants	-12.8	-87.4	-100.2
Post-2000 migrants	+21.5	+2.9	+24.3
Total	+8.7	-84.6	-75.9
	% GDP		
Pre-2001	-0.1	-0.8	-0.9
Post-2000	+0.2	+0.0	+0.2
Total	+0.1	-0.8	-0.7

Marginal cost scenario

	EEA	Non-EEA	Total
	£ billions (at 2011 prices)		
Pre-2001 migrants	+4.9	-41.4	-36.5
Post-2000 migrants	+35.2	+28.6	+63.8
Total	+40.2	-12.8	+27.3
	% GDP		
Pre-2001	+0.0	-0.4	-0.3
Post-2000	+0.3	+0.3	+0.6
Total	+0.4	-0.1	+0.3

Notes: Monetary quantities are at constant 2011 prices. Totals may not add because of rounding errors. Some of the quantities in this table differ very slightly from those given in Dustmann and Frattini (2013). This is because a slightly different deflator has been used to convert current prices to 2011 prices.

the latter scenario. Both trajectories exhibit a sharp deterioration in the fiscal balance following the financial crisis. In 2009-10, the balance for UK natives was around –£2,500 per head in 2011 prices. This is about mid-way between the two estimates for pre-2001 migrants. It is much worse than the estimates for recent migrants.

Table 4.2 shows the fiscal balances of various types of migrant over the period 2001-2011 as a whole.[6] EEA and non-EEA migrants are shown separately. The total net contribution of all migrants over this period ranges from -£76 billion at 2011 prices under the average cost scenario to +£27 billion under the marginal cost scenario. These are large numbers in absolute terms, but they are only -0.7% and +0.3% of GDP respectively. For recent non-EEA migrants, the balance is between +£3 billion (< 0.1% of GDP) and +£29 billion (+0.2% of GDP), depending on the method of estimation. For recent EEA migrants, the balance is between +£22 billion (+0.2% of GDP) and +£35 billion (+0.2% of GDP). The surplus of £22 billion for EEA migrants under the average cost scenario is the figure which has hit the headlines in the national media.

Critique of Dustmann and Frattini

D&F's estimates have been criticised by the organisation Migration Watch UK (2014), mainly on the grounds that government revenue from recent migrants has been seriously overestimated. D&F also fail to explore the possible fiscal consequences of native job loss due to competition from migrants.[7]

Migration Watch claims that D&F exaggerate the earnings and wealth of recent migrants and take inadequate account of their demographic and economic characteristics. As a result, D&F overestimate the amount of revenue that the government receives from these migrants in the form of income tax, national insurance, VAT and other indirect taxes, company taxes and business rates, council tax and inheritance tax. Migration Watch also claims that D&F underestimate the amount of tax credits and housing benefit that recent migrants receive.

Dustmann and Frattini (2014b) have responded to these claims by saying that Migration Watch has misunderstood their method for allocating income tax and national insurance. Elsewhere, they tacitly concede (Dustmann and Frattini, 2013b) that they may have exaggerated the amount of tax paid by recent migrants in the form of corporation tax, capital gains tax and business rates. They make no mention of other items, such as indirect taxes, council tax, inheritance tax, tax credits and housing benefit.

Migration Watch quantifies the effect of these supposed errors in the D&F paper and suggests various adjustments to their average cost estimates. Over the period 2001-2011 as a whole, these adjustments come to an estimated total of £52 billion in current prices. If we exclude the disputed adjustment for personal taxes (income tax and national insurance) the total is still £41 billion. This is a large amount and its accuracy is difficult to judge. However, it is sufficiently large and the supporting evidence is sufficiently strong to believe that Migration Watch is on to something.

Public goods under the marginal cost scenario

In an appendix to its critique, Migration Watch criticises the marginal cost scenario of D&F for its treatment of public goods. D&F classify interest on the national debt and also expenditure on 'economic affairs' (transport, energy, communication and construction etc) as pure public goods which are ascribed entirely to the native population under the marginal cost scenario. Migration Watch argues that such expenditures are significantly larger because of recent immigration and should be ascribed to migrants in proportion to their population share, even under the marginal cost scenario. This argument is defensible in the case of economic affairs, but not for debt interest. Government interest payments should only be ascribed to migrants for debt incurred as a result of their arrival or presence in the UK. As Williams (2013) points out, even in the absence of recent migrants, the government would have had to pay interest on the debts incurred before their arrival. The purpose of the marginal cost scenario is not to assess whether or not the fiscal contribution of recent migrants is fair. This is the task of the average cost scenario. The purpose of the marginal cost scenario is to assess what is the impact of recent migrants on government finances.

Using marginal cost accounting, it appears that recent migrants generated a small fiscal surplus during their initial years in the UK. As a result, the national debt and government interest payments grew more slowly than they would have done in the absence of these migrants. Under marginal cost accounting, this should be registed as a credit on the migrant account. It was only after the financial crisis that the government borrowed a significant amount on behalf of recent migrants. Simulations described in Appendix 1 suggest that the resulting interest flows were relatively small and their inclusion would not materially affect the outcome. The conclusion is that D&F were broadly correct to exclude debt interest payments under their marginal cost scenario.

Labour displacement

It is conventional in the literature on fiscal impact to assume that competition from migrants has no effect at all on the level of native employment. This would be true if labour markets were perfect and wages adjusted instantly to price all workers into employment. However, recent experience indicates that this is not the situation in the UK. Real wages fell in the wake of the financial crisis, but this did not prevent a reduction in native employment. Between 2007 and 2011, the number of UK natives in employment fell by 700,000, or nearly 3%. Given that wages did not adjust fast enough to price native workers back into a job, it is reasonable to assume that immigration had at least a temporary impact on the level of native employment. D&F recognise this possibility in a footnote, but they do not explore its potential fiscal implications.

Evidence on the displacement of UK native workers was reviewed in Chapter 2. To illustrate the potential fiscal impact of displacement I have done some simple calculations. They refer only to recent migrants. It must be stressed that these calculations are not estimates in any scientific sense, and are designed merely to illustrate the possible orders of magnitude involved. The key steps involved in these calculations are as follows:

- For each 100 extra jobs obtained by recent migrants during the pre-crisis years 2001-2007, there is assumed to be a durable loss of 10 native jobs; and for each 100 extra jobs obtained by such migrants during the recession years 2008-2011 there is a durable loss of 20 native jobs. Thus, if a native job is lost in a particular year due to migrant competition this loss is not made up within the period covered by the estimates. These assumptions have some support in the literature but many economists would dispute them. They imply that native employment is approximately 270,000 or 1.1% less in 2011 than it would have been in the absence of recent migration.

- *Fiscal cost.* The loss of native jobs due to migration means that natives pay fewer taxes and receive more benefits than would otherwise be the case. The resulting cost to the exchequer is estimated by assuming that the average amount lost to the exchequer for each native job lost is equal to 40% of government revenue per native in employment in the given year. The following is an example. The amount of government revenue ascribed by D&F to natives in 2011 was £462 billion,[8] and the number of natives in employment was 25.0 million. Dividing yields almost £18,500 for average revenue per UK native in employment. Forty per cent of this figure is £7,400. This is the amount which is assumed to be lost to the exchequer in 2011 for the average native worker without a job due to competition from recent migrants. This is a crude approach but the order of magnitude is probably correct. For comparison, in 2013 the fiscal loss resulting from job loss by a single adult, without children and working a 40 hour week for the minimum wage was in the range £4,400-£9,900, depending on age and living arrangements. A similar method of estimation was used for other years.

- *Reassignment.* The final step is to re-assign part of government net revenue (revenue minus expenditure) from recent migrants to the native population. The amount re-assigned from any particular migrant group depends on the assumed amount of native labour displaced by migrants from this group.

The effect of reassignment is to reduce the fiscal surplus generated by recent migrants. For the period 2001-2011 as a whole, the total amount re-assigned is approximately £10.5 billion (at 2011 prices).

The overall effect of adjustments

Figures 4.2a to 4.2d show the combined effect of the various adjustments described above. The adjustments include all Migration Watch adjustments excluding those for debt interest and personal taxes (income tax and national insurance). They also include an adjustment for native labour displacement and my own estimate of the migrant share of debt interest. Table 4.3 gives details of how these adjustments affect the fiscal balance over the period 2001-2011 as a whole. In all cases, the illustrative adjustment for labour displacement is relatively small and does not greatly affect the results. The adjustment for debt interest payment is even smaller. It is interesting to note that this adjustment is positive for recent EEA migrants. For most of the period, these migrants generated a fiscal surplus (however measured), thereby reducing the need for government borrowing. The resulting reduction in government interest payments is credited to EEA migrants as a plus item in Table 4.3.

Figure 4.2b plots the fiscal balance for recent EEA migrants as estimated by D&F using the average cost method. It also plots this balance taking into account the various adjustments described above. The adjusted balance is positive up to 2007 and then goes into deficit during the recession. Figure 5.2b repeats the same exercise using the marginal cost method. In this case, the adjusted balance is positive for most of the time and close to zero during the recession. Over the period 2001-2011 as a whole, before adjustment, the balance for recent EEA migrants is +£22 billion (average cost method) and +£35 billion (marginal cost method). After adjustment these become -£0.3 billion and +£9.5 billion respectively. Thus, the large 2001-2011 surplus which D&F find for recent EEA migrants, and about which there has been so much publicity, is either smaller or non-existent, depending on how it is measured.

Figures 4.2c and 4.2d repeat the same exercise for non-EEA migrants. With the average cost method, the adjusted balance for these migrants is in almost continuous deficit. This deficit increases sharply during the recession. With the marginal cost method, the adjusted balance is close to zero right up to 2007, after which it deteriorates sharply. Depending on which of these methods is used to estimate it, the adjusted balance of non-EEA migrants during the recession is between -£2,000 and -£3,000 per capita. This is similar to that of UK natives (Figure 4.2d). Over the period 2001-2011 as a whole, before adjustment, the balance for recent non-EEA migrants is +£3 billion (average cost method) and +£28 billion (marginal cost method). After adjustment these become -£30 billion and -£20 billion respectively.

Figure 4.2a: Fiscal balances of recent EEA migrants (average cost method, £ per capita at 2011 prices)

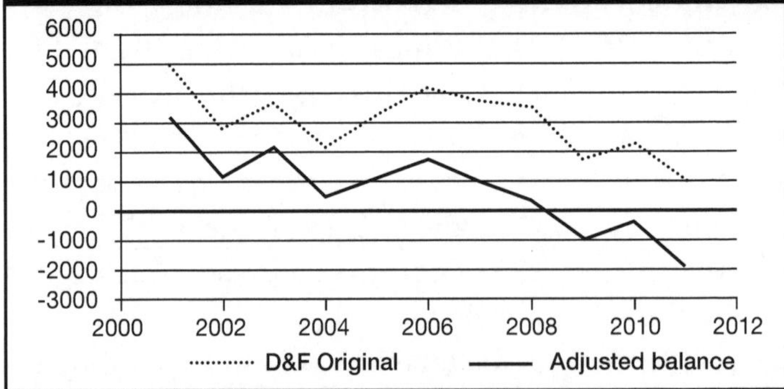

Figure 4.2b: Fiscal balances of recent EEA migrants (marginal cost method, £ per capita at 2011 prices)

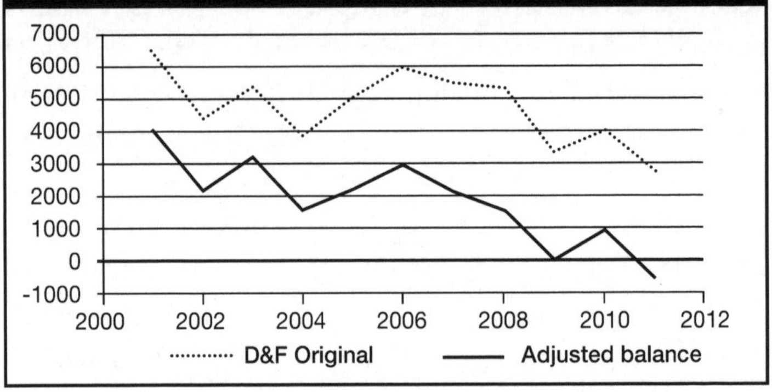

Figure 4.2c: Fiscal balances of recent non-EEA migrants (average cost method, £ per capita at 2011 prices)

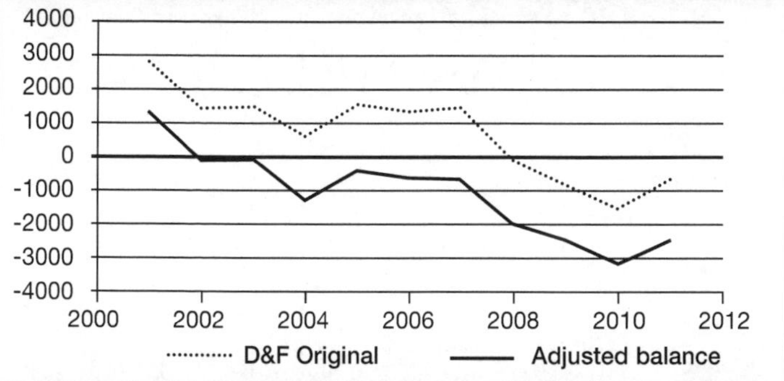

Figure 4.2d: Fiscal balances of recent non-EEA migrants (marginal cost method, £ per capita at 2011 prices)

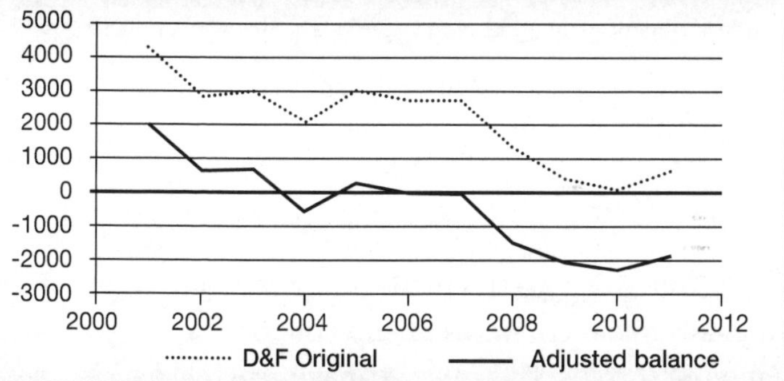

Table 4.3: Balance of revenue minus expenditure for recent migrants: total 2001-2011 with adjustments

	Average cost scenario £ billions (at 2011 prices)			**Marginal cost scenario** £ billions (at 2011 prices)		
	EEA	**Non-EEA**	**Total**	**EEA**	**Non-EEA**	**Total**
Original D&F balance	+21.5	+2.9	+24.3	+35.2	+28.6	+63.8
Revised MW adjustment*	-17.6	-26.3	-43.8	-23.6	-40.0	-63.6
Labour displacement adjustment	-4.2	-6.3	-10.5	-4.2	-6.3	-10.5
Interest adjustment**	n. a.	n. a.	n. a.	+2.0	-0.4	+1.6
Adjusted balance	-0.3	-29.7	-30.0	+9.5	-18.2	-8.7

Table 4.3: Balance of revenue minus expenditure for recent migrants: total 2001-2011 with adjustments

	Average cost scenario % GDP			Marginal cost scenario % GDP		
	EEA	Non-EEA	Total	EEA	Non-EEA	Total
Original D&F balance	+0.20	+0.03	+0.22	+0.32	+0.26	+0.59
Revised MW adjustment*	-0.16	-0.24	-0.40	-0.22	-0.37	-0.58
Labour displacement adjustment	-0.04	-0.06	-0.10	-0.04	-0.06	-0.10
Interest adjustment**	n.a.	n.a.	n.a.	+0.02	-0.00	+0.01
Adjusted balance	-0.00	-0.27	-0.28	+0.09	-0.17	-0.08

Note: Note: totals may not add because of rounding errors.
*The revised MW adjustment includes all Migration Watch adjustments except those for personal taxes (income tax and national insurance) and debt interest. Under the marginal cost scenario, these adjustments include the assignment to migrants of their pro rata share of government expenditure on economic affairs.
**The migrant share of interest on the national debt under the marginal cost scenario is estimated as described in Appendix 1.

Conclusions from the critique

Depending on the method of estimation, recent EEA migrants to the UK have either paid their way or generated a modest surplus. They may not have generated such a large fiscal surplus as D&F claim, but neither have they been a significant drain on the exchequer. Before the economic crisis their adjusted fiscal balance was always positive and the deterioration in this balance during the recession occurred alongside a general deterioration in government finances. Their per capita fiscal balance was consistently significantly more favourable than that of UK natives. The picture was less rosy for non-EEA migrants. However, the situation should improve for both types of migrant provided the economic recovery continues and provided the government's deficit reduction strategy remains on track. Expenditure on everyone, including migrants, will be squeezed and revenue will increase. Moreover, to the extent they exist, labour displacement effects should be starting to fade as native workers get jobs in the more buoyant demand conditions. As a result, the fiscal contribution of recent EEA migrants, properly measured, should return to surplus, if it has not already done so. The fiscal balance of recent non-EEA migrants, properly measured, is likely to remain in deficit.

Over the longer term, other factors will come into play as those migrants who remain in the UK acquire more family responsibilities and eventually retire from the labour force. Judging by observed migration flows, many EEA immigrants will return home before either point is reached, whereas most immigrants from the poorer members of the non-EEA grouping will remain permanently in the UK. To obtain a complete picture would require an assessment of the future life trajectories of the migrants and their descendants. The outcome of such an exercise is uncertain. However, some indication is provided in a recent paper by Ruist (2014) who uses a dynamic life-cycle approach to estimate the future fiscal contribution of EU10 immigrants in Sweden. The EU10 consists mainly of former communist countries and includes Bulgaria and Romania, whose citizens have enjoyed free access to the Swedish labour market since these countries joined the EU. The author finds that the discounted net fiscal contribution of immigrants from these countries may be positive or negative depending on their income assimilation rates and on future real interest rates. The situation is unlikely to be very different here.

Office for Budget Responsibility projections

The Office for Budget Responsibility (OBR) in its 2013 Fiscal Responsibility Report produced long range projections of the fiscal consequences of migration.[9] In an appendix to the report there is a chart showing the projected ratio of the public sector net debt to GDP under various assumptions about migration. The assumed tax and expenditure policies are the same under all projections. If there is no migration at all, the debt-to-GDP ratio balloons from under 80% in 2012-13 to around 160% in 2062-63. With migration of 260,000 p. a. the debt-to-GDP ratio remains roughly constant at around 80%. This contrast has been used in the media and elsewhere as an argument for large-scale immigration as the only practical way to avoid a severe debt crisis.[10] This is misleading. Elsewhere in its report the OBR uses a different approach which suggests that, beyond a certain level, the fiscal benefits of further immigration are quite small.

Table 4.4 shows the OBR estimates of the fiscal gap under different migration assumptions. The fiscal gap is the immediate and durable increase in taxes or reduction in government expenditure required to achieve some target debt-to-GDP ratio by a certain date. Suppose the objective is to reduce the debt to 40% of GDP by 2062-63. The OBR estimates that to achieve this objective in the complete absence of migration (natural change projection) would require an immediate and durable increase in taxes or reduction in expenditure equivalent to 2.6% of GDP. Under this scenario the population in 2062 is 63.8 million, which is only a little higher than at the start of the projection period. With high net migration of 260,000 the required tax increase or expenditure reduction is equivalent to 0.7% of GDP. Under this scenario the population in 2062 is equal to 86.6 million. Comparing the two projections, the switch from no migration at all to high migration saves the taxpayer an annual amount equivalent to 1.9% of GDP. The extra population resulting from this switch is 22.8 million.

Table 4.4: OBR fiscal gap estimates

			Required adjustment to primary balance (% of GDP)		
Target year			2064–2065	2064–2065	2064–2065
Target debt-to-GDP ratio (%)			20	40	60
	Annual net migration	Population 2065 (millions)			
OBR high net migration	225,000	84.9	1.1	0.7	0.2
OBR central projection	165,000	80.6	1.5	1.1	0.6
OBR low net migration	105,000	76.4	1.9	1.4	1.0
High migration minus low migration	+120,000	+8.5	-0.8	-0.7	-0.8

The above comparison is not of great relevance to the current UK debate on migration. No-one is talking about stopping migration entirely. A more useful comparison is between different rates of positive net migration. Under the OBR high migration projection the rate of net migration is 120,000 p.a. higher than under its central projection. The eventual annual saving to the taxpayer from this additional migration is 0.5% of GDP. This gain must be set against the environmental and other costs of absorbing an extra 9.1 million into the population by 2062 resulting from the switch to high migration. Such extra population would be over and above the large increase in population that occurs under the central projection (approximately 14 million). Moreover, to preserve the 0.5% of GDP gain for the taxpayer would require continued net migration at the higher rate beyond 2062 with consequent impact on future population growth. A more recent report by the OBR implies a somewhat larger benefit from migration. It estimates that an extra 120,000 p.a. migrants would lead to an extra 8.1 million population by 2065 and an eventual annual saving to the taxpayer equal to 0.7% to 0.8% GDP.[11]

The OBR report is impressive. It is also frank about its limitations. Migrants are assumed to have the same economic characteristics as natives of the same age and gender (same productivity, same employment rate, same earnings, etc). Women of foreign birth are also assumed to have the same age specific fertility as native women. The fiscal benefits of immigration in the OBR analysis derive entirely from its impact on the age structure of the national population and on the ability of the UK government to shift certain fiscal costs onto foreign countries. Immigrants are on average relatively young when they arrive and have a long working life ahead of them during which many of them will pay more taxes than they receive in the form of government expenditure. Eventually, when they retire they will become a net burden on the exchequer but that will be many years in the future. A similar rejuvenating effect could be achieved over the medium term by raising the native birth rate. However, this would take longer and would be more costly. Immigration also provides the UK government with a cheap and ready supply of taxable workers. To raise and educate a native worker costs the government a great deal of money before any tax revenue is generated. In the case of immigrants, many of these costs are incurred in their home country before they arrive in the UK. Thus, some of the fiscal benefits of immigration in the OBR analysis are merely a disguised transfer to the UK government from taxpayers and families in other countries.

Some of the assumptions underlying the OBR migration analysis are open to question. For example, age- and gender-specific employment rates amongst the foreign-born population are currently somewhat lower than those of the native population, although this gap is likely to close if EU immigration continues at a high rate. Moreover, fertility rates are not the same. In 2011, non-UK born women had a total fertility rate of 2.28 as compared to 1.89 for UK born women. If this differential were to persist, it would have a substantial impact on the growth rate of population associated with any given level of net migration. By boosting the future working age population, it would also increase the age-related fiscal benefit of net migration. However, there is also a factor working in the opposite direction. The immigrants that have the highest total fertility rates tend to be those with the lowest employment rates, partly because fewer men are able to find jobs and partly because many of the women are occupied full-time at home. The major examples are people of African, Pakistani or Bangladeshi origin. They may have more children than the rest of the population - which is a potential fiscal benefit for the future if these children find gainful employment - but they are also less likely to be employed and hence more likely to be a net burden on the exchequer.

Taking everything into account, it seems likely that the OBR migration projections underestimate the impact of migration on UK population growth. These projections may also overestimate the beneficial effect of migration on public finances, although a lot depends on where the immigrants come from and on how well they and their children integrate into the UK labour market.

The OBR's 2015 report concludes a discussion of migration with the following warning:

> These scenarios should not be construed as an argument that the government needs to pursue a particular policy towards immigration in order to achieve (or avoid) a particular outcome for the public finances. Governments doubtless choose their policies towards immigration for a whole variety of social and economic reasons and they could choose to offset their direct fiscal impact with tax and spending policy decisions. [12]

Conclusion

There is widespread agreement amongst specialists that the overall fiscal impact of large-scale immigration is normally small as a proportion of GDP. The large positive fiscal contribution of some types of immigrant is largely or wholly offset by the negative contribution of others. Dustmann and Frattini (2013) estimate that over the period 2001-2011, migrants made a net fiscal contribution in the range -0.7% to +0.2% of GDP, depending on how it is measured. Their widely publicised claim that recent (post-2000) migrants from the EEA have generated a large fiscal surplus should be seen in perspective. The estimated surplus of £22 billion over the 2001-2011 is only 0.2% of GDP. Moreover, this may be an overestimate.

Simulations in the OBR report have been widely used in support of large-scale immigration. In fact, these simulations are designed to explore one specific issue, namely the fiscal benefits of rejuvenation through immigration. To this end the authors make specific assumptions about the economic and social characteristics of immigrants that may not hold in practice. In the OBR analysis, large-scale immigration leads to a small increase in the share of the national population who are of working age. The authors assume that this would result in an equivalent increase in the share of employed persons in the national population, and hence in the ratio of tax revenue to government expenditure and the ratio of total output to population (GDP per capita). These small benefits are achieved at the cost of rapid population growth. Moreover, it is highly uncertain whether even these small benefits would actually materialise in practice, given our lack of knowledge about the productivity, employment rates and earnings of the many millions of future migrants foreseen under the OBR projections.

It is worth stressing that the benefits of immigration, to the extent they exist, derive in part from the unrequited transfer of investments in human capital that were made in foreign countries before the immigrants arrived in the UK. Some of the fiscal benefits are merely a disguised transfer to the UK government from taxpayers and families in other countries. This effect is intensified by policies which focus on the attraction of highly skilled immigrants, who embody a great deal of human capital, to the exclusion of less skilled migrants.

Conclusions

The focus of this book has been on the economic and demographic consequences of large-scale immigration. Some of these consequences are negative for the existing population of the UK and their descendants, others are potentially positive. If net migration continues on the present scale, the UK will quite soon have a much larger population and a much larger economy than would otherwise be the case, thereby imposing new pressures on the environment and national infrastructure especially in London and the south-east of the country. Some of these pressures can be eased with advance planning and public investment, but others cannot. For example, if controls over building on the green belt are relaxed, this will encourage more house-building and help to ease the immigration-driven shortage of housing, but only at the cost of a permanent loss of amenity for the existing population of these areas.

The potential economic benefits of large-scale immigration stem mainly from its impact on the national age structure. Large-scale immigration helps to rejuvenate an ageing UK population by importing a large number of young migrants, thereby increasing the share of the population who are of working age. Providing these potential workers get jobs without displacing natives, and providing they are sufficiently productive and well-paid, this will increase GDP per capita and generate a fiscal surplus for the government. However, such benefits are by no means guaranteed, and even if they do materialise they will be small. The outcome depends on the skills of immigrants and on their integration into the UK labour market. If many of the immigrants fail to get jobs, or if they end up in low skill jobs or displace native workers, large-scale immigration will have a negative impact on GDP per capita and on government finances. Thus, the impact could be positive or negative, but either way it is unlikely to be very large. The only thing that is certain is that immigration on the present scale, if it continues, will lead eventually to a much larger population and a much larger total GDP than would otherwise be the case, with consequent pressure on infrastructure and the environment.

'Tens of thousands'

There is a widespread concern that immigration is too high and is out of control. David Cameron has responded to this concern by saying that his government aims to reduce overall net migration to 'tens of thousands' a year.[1] The scale of this task is clear from the preliminary estimates of migration by citizenship shown in Table 6.1. In the year ending March 2015, overall net migration was 330,000. To cut this figure to 90,000 would require a reduction of 240,000 in annual net migration. Where might this reduction come from? The government has little control over the migration of British and other EU citizens. If net migration of British and EU citizens were to remain at the levels shown in Table 5.1, the required reduction of 240,000 in net migration would have to come entirely from citizens of non-EU countries. In the year covered by this table, some 284,000 non-EU citizens entered the UK as long-term migrants and 88,000 left the UK. Assuming no change in the number leaving, it would require an 85% (240,000) reduction in the number of non-EU citizens entering the UK to achieve the net migration target. The result would be an annual outflow of 88,000 non-EU citizens as compared to an inflow of 44,000. Such a huge reduction in the inflow would be virtually impossible to achieve and any serious attempt to do so would cause outrage amongst those affected, both in the UK and abroad. It would severely damage our economy and our diplomatic ties with other countries.

Table 5.1: UK migration by citizenship, year ending March 2015 (thousands)

	All citizen-ships	British	Non-British	EU	Non-EU	New Common-wealth	Other Foreign
Inflow	636	83	553	269	284	90	194
Outflow	307	132	174	86	88	24	64
Balance (net migration)	+ 330	- 49	+ 379	+ 183	+196	+ 66	+130

Non-EU migrants

Official migration policy differentiates sharply between EU and non-EU migrants. A whole raft of measures has been introduced to reduce the scale of immigration from non-EU countries and shape it in ways that are more beneficial to the UK. Some of these measures build on initiatives by the last Labour government during its closing years in office.

Long-term migrants from most non-EU countries are now subject to quite strict visa requirements.[2] There is a tier system which gives preference to skilled migrants and entrepreneurs. It also permits certain international students to remain in the country at the end of their studies. Controls over student visas have been tightened and many educational institutions catering to immigrants have been closed. There are also temporary visas for unskilled migrants in occupations where there is a shortage of domestic applicants. In addition, there are now financial tests to ensure that migrants entering by the family route do not become a burden on the welfare state.

These restrictions have had a significant impact on immigration from outside the EU. Net migration from the mostly poor countries that belong to the New Commonwealth has fallen sharply to a provisional estimate of 66,000 in the year ending March 2015. This fall is partly due to the clamp-down on the entry of students who are believed to bogus. However, after a period of decline, net migration from other non-EU countries has recently increased to a provisional estimate of 130,000.

EU migrants

The main obstacle to the achievement of David Cameron's target is the high level of immigration from our EU partners. Migration from these countries is subject to few restrictions.[3] The government plans to restrict their initial access to welfare benefits, but this is unlikely to have a dramatic impact. The main driver of migration is the difference in wage rates and job opportunities between the UK and many countries in eastern and southern Europe. There is also the attraction of in-work benefits as a wage supplement for employed migrants in the UK. Another factor is the growth of a migrant diaspora. As more people from the sending countries establish themselves in the UK, there is a growth of migrant communities which provide support networks for new migrants. This reduces the cost and risk of migration, thus encouraging further migration. This is known as chain migration.

The high rate of immigration from eastern and southern Europe will only decline significantly when either (1) these countries draw much closer to the UK in terms of wage rates and job opportunities, or else (2) severe restrictions are placed on the flow of labour from these countries. David Cameron has ruled out the latter option,[4] so what happens to EU migration will depend mainly on how well the economies of eastern and southern Europe perform. If their economies grow rapidly in the future, fewer people will leave them to seek work in the UK and immigration from these countries will begin to fall. Some clue as to what may happen is provided by IMF forecasts for medium-term growth up to 2020.[5] These forecasts are mostly optimistic about the first wave of former communist countries to join the EU, and it is likely that net migration from these countries will begin tailing off within a few years. Forecasts for southern Europe and the poorer eastern states, such as Bulgaria and Romania, are mixed and migration from these countries is unlikely to fall dramatically any time soon.

There is also the issue of future entrants to the EU. David Cameron has floated the idea that labour mobility should be restricted until per capita income in a new member state has reached a given, rather high, percentage of the EU average.[6] The theory is that once this level is reached there will be only a weak incentive for migration, so that controls can be lifted without provoking a flood of inward migration. David Cameron has also threatened to veto the entry of new EU members unless the rules governing labour mobility are modified to allow the richer countries more control over migration flows from the new entrants.[7] Whether anything will come of this threat remains to be seen.

Moral responsibilities[8]

Migration policy is not just about national interest to be pursued without regard to its impact on the rest of the world. The moral strength of the open borders lobby derives from the fact that most of the people who are kept out by immigration controls are not criminals or welfare scroungers. They are people seeking the opportunity to make a better life for themselves and their families through honest work. Some risk their lives for this opportunity.

In political terms, the demand for open borders is a non-starter. The resulting scale of immigration would almost certainly be enormous. According to a Gallup World Poll survey 32% of the entire population of Sub-Saharan Africa would emigrate permanently if they had the opportunity.[9] Their second most preferred destination was the UK. This percentage is equivalent to 308 million people wanting to leave in 2015, rising to a projected 685 million by 2050 because of population growth.[10] If only a small fraction of these people actually left and came to the UK the result would be an inflow of tens of millions. In addition there would be many millions from the Middle East and South Asia. It is unrealistic to believe that the UK electorate would accept immigration on this scale. For better or worse, the UK is still a democracy and it still has sovereign control over the bulk of non-EU migration. Public hostility would either prevent the implementation of a comprehensive open borders policy or force its abandonment.

As a compromise, the economist Dani Rodrik has suggested that rich countries should implement a *temporary* work visa scheme that would expand their total labour force by no more than a fixed percentage.[11] He suggests 3%, which in the UK case would be around 1 million. Under the scheme a mix of skilled and unskilled workers from poor countries would be allowed to fill jobs in the rich countries for a maximum of five years. To ensure that the workers return home at the end of their contracts, the programmes would be supported by a range of carrots and sticks applied by both home and host countries. As the original migrants return home, a new wave of workers from the same countries would replace them. If all rich countries were to implement such a scheme, Roderik estimates there would be a direct gain for the world economy equal to $360 billion annually. This figure takes no account of the additional benefits in form of know-how, skills, networks and savings that returning migrants would bring to their home countries.

Rodrik's scheme is a good idea in theory. The fixed upper limit on the stock of temporary workers in a host country at any one time would limit the impact of the scheme on total population. The mixture of skilled and unskilled migrants would minimise disruption in the local labour market, especially if the scheme were implemented gradually over a period of years. The main practical difficulty would be to ensure that the temporary workers actually leave the country at the end of the stipulated period. Rodrik believes that with appropriate financial carrots and sticks, this objective could be achieved. However, there would inevitably be leakages as supposedly temporary migrants found ways to settle permanently in the host country, by for example marrying locals or using human rights law to obstruct enforcement of the rules.[12] The scale of such leakages is difficult to judge in advance. The answer depends on the willingness of future governments and the courts to formulate and enforce the rules required for the temporary worker scheme to operate effectively. The danger is that such a scheme might unravel as governments create ever more exceptions and the courts pick holes in the rules.

Quite apart from its impact on individual migrants and their families, migration has implications for the sending countries as a whole. This is a contentious issue amongst experts.[13] It is widely agreed that migration from a poor country to a rich country may bring certain benefits to the sending country. There is less agreement about the costs of migration to the sending country. On the plus side, migrants generate foreign exchange for the sending country through the transfer of remittances to their families back home. Moreover, the prospect of migration may encourage young people to study and acquire skills that will be useful in the prospective host country. In the event, many of these students may not emigrate but remain as skilled workers in their home country. Migrants who acquire skills abroad may also return and use their skills at home. Finally, emigration may stimulate the formation of international ties which are of benefit to the country of origin.

The benefits which poor countries derive from emigration must be set against its costs. These costs are mostly associated with the loss of skilled workers and entrepreneurs – the so-called 'brain drain'. If poor countries export skilled labour to rich countries, they may lose scarce professionals who are hard to replace. They may also lose the brightest and most dynamic of their potential leaders, those who would normally build and sustain the institutions required for development (Kapur and McHale, 2005). The gain to the rich countries that admit such people may be comparatively small, but for a poor sending country the loss may sometimes be considerable.

This is a familiar theme in the case of very poor countries in such areas as sub-Saharan Africa, but there are examples closer to home. There has been a massive outflow of doctors in recent times from Romania to other EU countries. Within a two-year period, around 30% of resident doctors left Romania, reducing the overall number of physicians from 20,000 in 2011 to 14,000 in 2013.[14]

Opponents of open borders typically favour selective migration policies that give priority to skilled workers and entrepreneurs. Such policies are now widespread and there is intense competition amongst the rich countries to attract and retain skilled or talented individuals from around the globe. The UK Home Office, for example, operates a points-based system for migrants from outside the EEA or Switzerland. This system gives preference to 'high value' migrants and skilled workers and excludes most types of unskilled worker. The Home Office criteria do not explicitly mention country of origin, so in principle there could be a large flow into the UK of skilled professionals and the like from poor countries. In recognition of this possibility the NHS operates a code of practice which states that, with certain exceptions, developing countries should not be targeted when actively recruiting healthcare professionals.

The impact of migration on sending countries is a complex issue, and it would be inappropriate to impose a blanket ban on the recruitment of skilled labour from poor countries of the type operated by the NHS for healthcare professionals. However, where feasible, the potential impact of skilled labour migration on poor sending countries should be taken into account in the criteria for admission to the UK and eventual settlement here. More generally, UK policy towards migration from such countries should be designed so as to promote their wellbeing and economic development. It should be seen as a complement to our aid policy.

This raises the issue of students. A good way to help poor countries would be for the UK to expand the existing programme of bursaries for the higher education of students from these countries. In most cases the award of such bursaries should be conditional on students leaving the UK on completion of their studies. The policing of this aspect of the policy could be left to the host university or other educational institution. The fact that students are expected to leave the UK at the end of their studies would not in itself guarantee that they would actually go home. They might well go to another rich country such as the US. However, the scheme could be accompanied by financial and other inducements to make a return home attractive.

One problem with the above proposal is the following. During its initial phase the scheme would involve a large build-up in the stock of international students in the UK. This would show up in the statistics as a large increase in net migration. After a time the stock of international students participating in the scheme would stabilise, and the number of participants leaving the UK on completion of their studies would be broadly similar to the number of new participants entering the country. However, during the transition there would be a bulge in net migration. It is for this reason that some people have suggested that students should be excluded from the migration statistics. The alternative is to identify study-related migration in a symmetric fashion, so that the number of people who are leaving the country because their studies are complete can be compared to the number entering the country in order to study. The ONS now publishes such information.

Refugees

The UK is a signatory to the UN Refugee Convention. This convention defines a refugee as:

> A person who owing to a well-founded fear of being persecuted for reasons of race, religion, nationality, membership of a particular social group or political opinion, is outside the country of his nationality and is unable or, owing to such fear, is unwilling to avail himself of the protection of that country; or who, not having a nationality and being outside the country of

> his former habitual residence as a result of such events, is unable or, owing to such fear, is unwilling to return to it. [15]

According to the above definition a person may be simultaneously both an economic migrant and a refugee. The Syrians currently streaming through Greece and the Balkans towards northern Europe are frequently described as people fleeing persecution. This is misleading. It is true that many of them originally left Syria to escape persecution, but by the time they enter Europe they have previously found protection in Turkey or elsewhere, often in a refugee camp. They are economic migrants seeking a better life than they currently enjoy. However, according to the UN definition, they are still classified as refugees if it is unsafe for them to go back to Syria.

The number of individuals seeking asylum in the UK has risen in recent years, but the increase has been much less than in many other EU countries. In the second quarter of 2015, the UK processed 8,080 first-time asylum applications, of which 3,240 (40%) were successful.[16] The number of first-time asylum applications and success rates in other countries during this period were: Germany 46,085 (43%), France 19,425 (25%), Italy 13,760 (47%) and Sweden 10, 065 (75%). It is reported that 200,000 asylum seekers entered Germany in September 2015.[17] Despite their rapidly increasing number, Syrians still constitute only a quarter of all individuals seeking asylum in the EU as a whole.

There are two reasons why the number of people seeking asylum in the UK has remained low despite the huge influx into certain other EU countries: (1) government policy towards the entry of potential asylum seekers is restrictive, and (2) the UK is geographically isolated from continental Europe, making irregular entry difficult. As far as Syria is concerned, UK policy is to provide financial support for relief agencies operating in the Middle East, thereby helping to improve the quality of life of refugees currently located in the region and reduce their incentive to leave for Europe. It has also granted asylum to a modest number of Syrian nationals – approximately 5,000 between 2011 and mid-2015.[18] The government has promised to provide asylum over the next five years for an additional 20,000 Syrian refugees, mostly vulnerable individuals currently living in refugee camps.[19] It has declined to participate in a controversial German-inspired scheme of national quotas for distributing refugees who have already managed to enter the EU.

The refugee crisis facing Europe is serious and may get worse. As EU Council President Donald Tusk has warned:

> Conflicts in the Middle East will not end any time soon. Today we are talking about millions of potential refugees trying to reach Europe, not thousands. It is likely that more refugees will flow towards Europe, not less, especially as almost all of them feel invited to Europe. [20]

In addition to the factors pulling refugees towards Europe there is also the important push factor that conditions are getting worse for refugees in the countries where they are presently located. As the UNHCR notes:

> After years of rising pressure, the economies and infrastructure of many refugee-hosting countries are buckling, making it increasingly difficult for refugees to find work, shelter, health care, and education. As humanitarian appeals to assist them go underfunded, many simply move on. [21]

Quite apart from conflicts in the Middle East, there are also endemic conflicts in Afghanistan and Eritrea. Until these various conflicts are resolved, the flow of refugees towards Europe is likely to continue.

The EU countries are groping towards a collective approach to the refugee crisis. In September 2015, in the face of fierce opposition from certain countries, a national quota scheme for distributing 160,000 refugees was forced through by majority vote. The UK has an opt-out in this area of policy and has chosen not to participate in the scheme. The government view is that more effort should be made to resolve the conflicts that are creating refugees, and that more effort should be made to improve conditions in refugee camps and to support refugee-hosting countries in conflict regions. EU border controls should also be tightened so that asylum seekers can be speedily processed at their point of entry and individuals whose applications are denied can be speedily removed from the EU. These views are gaining support across the EU and various initiatives along these lines are in the pipeline or under consideration. Negotiations are under way to obtain the support of Turkey in helping to stem the flow of migrants. However, it will be some time before such initiatives take effect, and no-one can be sure how well they will work.

Tighter border controls and the speedier removal of failed asylum seekers may help to calm public disquiet, but they will do little to staunch the flow of genuine refugees into the EU. Greater funding for refugee camps and frontline states may encourage some refugees to stay put, but if the conflicts drag on many refugees will abandon hope of returning home and will head for Europe. If this happens, there will be growing moral and diplomatic pressure on the UK to accept more of them.

The impact of refugees on their host economy depends on their level of education, entrepreneurial capacity and integration in the labour market. These vary greatly depending on their country of origin. According to Statistics Sweden, more than 40% of Syrians in the country in 2014 had at least upper secondary education, compared to 20% of those from Afghanistan and 10% for those coming from Eritrea.[22] If this pattern holds for other host countries, it would suggest that the UK might benefit economically from the entry of more adult refugees from Syria. The self-interest case for admitting most other types of refugee is weaker. According to a recent OECD report, refugees in the EU typically find it hard to get a job and their employment rate is initially very low.[23] Most refugees eventually get a job but in the meantime they are supported by the taxpayer. This makes it important to promote the integration of refugees and help them to find employment.

Within reason we have a moral obligation to give asylum to genuine refugees. We also have an obligation to help those who are given asylum to find work commensurate with their skills, thereby making them useful members of our own society and enhancing their capacity to be useful if they eventually return home. It is legal under international law to require that refugees leave the host country when conditions have settled down in their country of origin and it is safe them to go home. This is a good idea in principle, but it should be applied with discretion. Refugees should not be forced to leave after they have been in the host country for many years and have put down roots there. They should be helped to go home should they so desire, but the choice should be theirs.

Appendix 1

The share of recent migrants in government interest payments under the marginal cost scenario

This appendix shows how the share of recent migrants in expenditure on government interest payments should be derived.

The mathematics

The primary balance of migrants in year t is equal to the government revenue they generate (taxes etc) minus the government expenditure ascribed to them (excluding interest). Mathematically, this can be expressed as follows:

(1) $P_t = R_t - E_t$

The current balance of migrants is equal to their primary balance minus the portion of government expenditure on interest payments that is ascribed to them:

(2) $P_t = P_r - I_t$

The migrants' portion of interest payments is equal to the rate of interest multiplied by their portion of the national debt inherited from the previous year:

(3) $I_t = r_t D_{t-1}$

The migrants' portion of national debt at the end of year t is equal to their portion of inherited national debt minus their current balance in year t:

(4) $D_t = D_{t-1} - C_t$

Note that measures the cumulative impact of migrants on the national debt. It is negative if migrants have generated a fiscal surplus in the past, thereby allowing the government to borrow less than it would otherwise have done.

To close the system we assume that the migrants' portion of national debt at the end of the year 2000 (beginning of the year 2001) is equal to zero:

(5) $D_{2000} = 0$

Application

Table A1 shows how the migrant portion of government expenditure on interest payments is calculated using the above formulae. The revenue and expenditure series used to construct this table were estimated using the D&F marginal cost method and include the revised Migration Watch and labour displacement adjustments. The interest rate was derived by dividing total government interest payments by total national debt as given by the House of Commons Library (Webb and Bardens, 2013).

To understand table A1, let us consider EEA migrants in 2001. These migrants have a primary balance equal to £0.34 billion. Since this is the first year they are in the UK, they inherit no national debt from the previous year and hence no government interest payments are ascribed to them. Their current balance is therefore equal to £0.34 billion. Government borrowing in 2001 is reduced by this amount, and national debt at the end of the year is £0.34 billon less than would otherwise be the case. This is indicated by the entry -£0.34 billion in the column headed 'Cumulative impact on national debt' in the table. Because national debt at the end of 2001 is smaller, the cost of servicing this debt in 2002 is reduced. This is indicated by the entry -£0.02 billion in the column headed 'Impact on government interest payments'. The migrants' current balance is found by deducting this item from their primary balance of £0.25 billion. Their current balance in 2002 is thus £0.25 billion – (-£0.02 billion) = £0.28 billion. The discrepancy in this equation is due to a rounding error.

The cumulative impact of such accounting is shown in the final line of Table A1. In the year 2011, government interest payments are £0.40 billion lower because of recent EEA migration and £0.54 billion higher because of recent non-EEA migration. The national debt at the end of 2011 is £8.42 billion smaller because of recent EEA migration and £18.01 billion larger because of recent non-EEA migration.

It is clear from Table A1 that interest is a small item in comparison with the primary balance. When interest is taken into account, the resulting current balance is always slightly better than the primary balance for recent EEA migrants and slightly worse towards the end of the period for recent non-EEA migrants.

Table A1: How government expenditure on interest should be ascribed to recent migrants under the marginal cost scenario

£ billions

Year	Recent EEA migrants				Recent Non-EEA migrants			
	Primary balance P_t	Impact on government interest payments I_t	Current balance C_t	Cumulative impact on national debt D_t	Primary balance P_t	Impact on government interest payments I_t	Current balance C_t	Cumulative impact on national debt D_t
2000	0	0	0	0	0	0	0	0
2001	0.34	0.00	0.34	-0.34	0.53	0.00	0.53	-0.53
2002	0.25	-0.02	0.28	-0.62	0.28	-0.04	0.31	-0.85
2003	0.51	-0.04	0.55	-1.16	0.44	-0.05	0.49	-1.34
2004	0.35	-0.07	0.42	-1.58	-0.56	-0.08	-0.48	-0.86
2005	0.82	-0.09	0.90	-2.48	0.29	-0.05	0.34	-1.19
2006	1.61	-0.14	1.75	-4.23	-0.03	-0.07	0.04	-1.23
2007	1.68	-0.24	1.92	-6.15	-0.13	0.07	-0.06	-1.17
2008	1.32	-0.30	1.62	-7.76	-3.08	-0.06	-3.02	1.85
2009	-0.21	-0.29	0.08	-7.84	-4.70	0.07	-4.77	6.62
2010	1.07	-0.35	1.42	-9.26	-5.59	0.30	-5.89	12.51
2011	-1.24	-0.40	-0.84	-8.42	-4.96	0.54	-5.50	18.01

Appendix 2

Sources

Table 1.1: Office for National Statistics, Long-Term International Migration, 27 November 2014, Table 2.03.

Table 1.2: Office for Budget Responsibility, 'Fiscal sustainability report', July 2013, Tables A2 and A3.

Table 1.3: Wadsworth, J. (2015), Table 3.

Table 3.1: Office for National Statistics, Population Projections, 2012-based.

Table 4.1: OECD, International Migration Outlook 2013, Table 3.7.

Table 4.4: OBR (2013), Table 5.1.

Table 5.1: Office for National Statistics, 'Provisional Long-term International Migration (LTIM) estimates, year ending September 2103', February 2014.

Figures 1.1 to 1.3: Office for National Statistics, 'Provisional Long-term International Migration (LTIM) estimates, year ending March 2015', 27 August 2015.

Figure 1.4: Department for Work and Pensions, 'National Insurance number allocations to adult overseas nationals entering the UK', Department for Work and Pensions, 27 February 2014.

Figures 2.1 to 2.2: Office for National Statistics, 'Labour market statistics summary data tables', Table 8, 11 July 2015.

Figures 3.1 to 3.2: Office for National Statistics, Population Projections, 2012-based.

Figures 4.2a to Figure 4.2d.3: Dustmann, C., and Frattini, T. (2013), Tables 4a and 4b.

Bibliography

Angrist, J. D. and Kugler, A. D. (2003), 'Protective or Counter-Productive? Labour Market Institutions and the Effect of Immigration on EU Natives', *Economic Journal*, vol. 113, no. 488, June, pp. F302-F331.

Booth, S., Howarth C., and Scarpetta, V. (2012), 'Tread carefully: The impact and management of EU free movement and immigration policy', Open Europe.

Borjas, G., J., Freeman, R. and Katz, L. F. (1997), 'How Much Do Immigration and Trade Affect Labour Market Outcomes', *Brookings Papers on Economic Activity*, I: pp. 1-90.

Borjas, G. J. (2001), 'Does Immigration Grease the Wheels of the Labor Market?', *Brookings Papers on Economic Activity*, 2001, pp. 69-119.

Borjas, G. J. (2013), 'Immigration and the American Worker: A Review of the Academic Evidence', *Backgrounder*, Center for Immigration Studies, April.

Card, D. (2001), 'Immigrant Inflows, Native Outflows and the Labor Market Impacts of Higher Immigration', *Journal of Labor Economics* 19(1):22-64.

Card, D. (2005), 'Is the New Immigration Really So Bad?' *The Economic Journal*. 115(507): pp. F300-F323.

Cebulla, A.,Daniel, M., and Zurawan, A. (2010), 'Spotlight on refugee integration: findings from the Survey of New Refugees in the United Kingdom', Summary of Research Report no. 37, Home Office, July.

Collier, P. (2003), *Exodus: How Migration Is Changing Our World*, London, Penguin Books.

Coleman, D. A. (2007), 'Time for a fresh start: the case for a UK Population Register', Submission to the House of Commons Treasury sub-Committee enquiry into Counting the Population.

Coleman, D. A. (2010), 'Projections of the ethnic minority populations of the United Kingdom 2006 – 2056.' *Population and Development Review* 36 no. 3, pp. 441- 486.

Dale, A., and Sameera, A. (2011), 'Marriage and employment patterns amongst UK-raised Indian, Pakistani, and Bangladeshi women', *Ethnic and Racial Studies*, Vol. 34, issue 6, pp. 902-924.

Devlin, C., Bolt, O., Patel. D., Harding, D. and Ishtiaq, H. (2014), 'Impacts of migration on UK native employment: An analytical review of the evidence', Home Office and Department for Business Innovation & Skills, Occasional Paper 109, March.

Dorling, D. (2013), *Population 10 Billion*, London, Constable.

Dustmann, C., F. Fabbri , I. Preston and Wadsworth, J. (2003), 'The local labour market effects of immigration in the UK', Home Office Online Report, 6 March.

Dustmann, C., Fabbri, F. and Preston, I. (2005), 'The Impact of Immigration on the British Labour Market', *Economic Journal*, vol. 115(507), F324-F341.

Dustmann, C., Frattini, T. and Preston, I. (2008), 'The effect of immigration along the distribution of wages'. CReAM Discussion Paper Series No. 0803, Centre for Research and Analysis of Migration (CReAM), Department of Economics, University College, London.

Dustmann, C., and Frattini, T. (2013a), 'The Fiscal Effects of Immigration to the UK', CReAM Discussion Paper Series No. 22/13, Centre for Research and Analysis of Migration (CReAM), Department of Economics, University College London.

Dustmann, C., and Frattini, T. (2013b), Further Response to Comments on 'The Fiscal Impact of Immigration on the UK', CReAM blog, 26 November.

Dustmann, C., and Frattini, T. (2014a), 'There are no "Schoolboy Errors" in our report', CReAM blog, 29 January.

Dustmann, C. and Frattini, T. (2014b), 'Further Response to Comments on "The Fiscal Impact of Immigration on the UK"', CReAM blog, 12 March.

Environment Agency (2008), 'Water Resources for England and Wales - Current State and Future Pressures', December.

Gibson, J., and McKenzie, D. (2011), 'Eight Questions About Brain Drain', *Journal of Economic Perspectives*', Vol. 25, No.3, pp. 107-128.

Glitz, A. (2012), 'The Labor Market Impact of Immigration: A Quasi-Experiment Exploiting Immigrant Location Rules in Germany', *Journal of Labor Economics*, vol.30, No. 1 (January 2012), pp. 175–213.

Goodhart, D. (2013), *The British Dream: Successes and Failures of Post-war Immigration*, London, Atlantic Books.

Gott, C., and Johnson, K. (2002), 'The Migrant Population in the UK: fiscal effects'. Home Office Research, Development and Statistics Directorate Occasional Paper No 77. London, Home Office.

Jean, S., and Jiménez, M. (2007), 'The unemployment impact of immigration in OECD countries', Economics Department Working Paper #563, OECD, Paris.

Kaldor, N., (1966), 'The Causes of the Slow Rate of Growth of the United Kingdom Economy: An Inaugural Lecture', Cambridge, Cambridge University Press.

Kapur, D., and McHale, J. (2005), 'The Global Migration of Talent: What Does it Mean for Developing Countries?' Centre for Global Development, Policy Brief, October.

Lemos, S., (2010), *Labour market effects of Eastern European migration in Wales*, University of Leicester, UK.

Longhi, S., NIjkamp, P., and Poot, J., (2008), 'Meta-Analysis of Empirical Evidence on the Labour Market Impacts of Immigration', University of Waikato, PSC Discussion Paper No 67.

Lucchino, P., Rosazza-Bondibene and Portes, J. (2012), 'Examining the Relationship between Immigrating and Unemployment Using National Insurance Number Registration Data', NIESR Discussion Paper No. 386, 9 January.

MAC (2012), *Analysis of the Impacts of Migration*, Migration Advisory Committee. January.

Manacorda, M., Manning, A., and Wadsworth, J., (2006), 'The Impact of Immigration on the Structure of Male Wages: Theory and Evidence from Britain', LSE, CEP Discussion Paper No 754.

Migration Watch UK (2014), 'An Assessment of the Fiscal Effects of Migration to the UK', Briefing Paper 1.37.

Nathan, M., (2011), 'The long term impacts of migration in British cities: Diversity, Wages, Employment and Prices', SERC Discussion Paper 67.

Nickell, S., and Saleheen, J., (2008), 'The Impact of Immigration on Occupational Wages: Evidence from Britain', Federal Reserve Bank of Boston, Working Paper No. 08-6.

OBR (2013), 'Fiscal sustainability report', Office for Budget Responsibility, July 2013.

OBR (2015), 'Fiscal sustainability report', Office for Budget Responsibility, July 2015.

ONS (2014), 'Quality of Long-Term International Migration estimates from 2001 to 2011', Office for National Statistics, 27 February.

Ottaviano, G. I. P., and Peri , G., (2012), 'Rethinking the Effects of Immigration on Wages', *Journal of the European Economic Association*, 10:152-197.

Rodrik, D, (2011), *The Globalization Paradox*, Oxford, Oxford University Press.

Rowthorn, B., (2003), 'Migration Limits', *Prospect Magazine*, Issue 83, February.

Rowthorn, R. (2006), 'Cherry-Picking: A Dubious Practice', *Around the Globe*, Vol. 3, no.2, Spring: 17-23, Institute for the Study of Global Movements, University of Monash.

Rowthorn, R. E. (2008), 'The Fiscal Impact of Immigration on the Advanced Economies', *Oxford Review of Economic Policy*, Volume 24, Number 3, 2008, pp.560–580.

Ruhs, M. (2013), *The Price of Rights: Regulating International Labor Migration*, Princeton N.J., Princeton University.

Ruist, J. (2014), 'Free Immigration and Welfare Access: The Swedish Experience', *Fiscal Studies*, Vol. 35, no.1, pp. 19-39.

Smith, J and B. Edmonton (eds) (1997), *The New Americans: Economic, Demographic and Fiscal Effects of Immigration*, Washington DC: National Research Council; National Academy Press.

Sriskandarajah, D., Cooley, L., and Reed, H. (2005), 'Paying their way: The fiscal contribution of immigrants in the UK', London, IPPR, April.

Stone, M. (2013), 'Plain Assumptions and Unexplained Wizardry Called in Aid of "The Fiscal Effects of Immigration to the UK"', Civitas, London.

Wadsworth, J. (2015), 'Immigration and the UK Labour Market'. Centre for Economic Performance, LSE.

Williams, N. (2013), 'Responding to the Fiscal Effects of Immigration to the UK', Civitas, London.

Notes

Overview

1 Robert Rowthorn (2014), 'Large-scale Immigration: Its economic and demographic consequences for the UK', Civitas, August.

2 The demographer David Coleman (2010) provides a good analysis of the impact of immigration on the future ethnic and racial composition of the UK.

3 The European Economic Area = European Union plus Iceland, Liechtenstein and Norway.

Chapter 1

1 The ONS revisions cover overall net migration each year during the period 2001-2011. No breakdown of these revisions by area or into inflows and outflows is available.

2 Bulgaria and Romania are classified as EU from 2007 onwards and as non-EU before then.

3 ONS Population by Country of Birth and Nationality, 2013.

4 I was unable to find hard evidence for this statement. However, there is some indirect evidence in the case of trans-border marriages involving UK women and men from Pakistan or Bangladesh. The traditional custom is for brides in these countries to join their husband's household after marriage. Such a custom would involve a UK bride moving to Pakistan or Bangladesh if her husband was located there. However, it is now fairly common for a husband from Pakistan or Bangladesh to join his bride in the UK (Dale and Sameera, 2011). It is reasonable to assume that such a frequent break with custom has an economic motive.

5 Youth unemployment rate = the number of unemployed people aged 15 to 24 as a percentage of the active population of the same age. Unemployed persons are those who (1) are not employed; (2) are available to start work within the next two weeks; (3) have actively sought employment at some time during the previous for weeks. Source: http://ec.europa.eu/eurostat/statistics-explained/index.php/File:Table_1_Youth_unemployment,_2014 Q4_%28%25%29.png.

6 The percentages are taken from Eurostat: http://ec.europa.eu/eurostat/tgm/table.do?tab=table&init=1&language=en&pcode=tec00114&plugin=1.

7 '"Wave" of Polish immigration is over, says ambassador – these days Poles prefer to stay at home', *The Independent*, 22 April 2014.

8 The number of NINo registrations of Polish nationals was 80,467 in 2012, 111,449 in 2013 and 97,417 in 2014. Source: https://www.gov.uk/government/statistics/national-insurance-number-allocations-to-adult-overseas-nationals-entering-the-uk-to-december-2014

9 Office for National Statistics, 'Bulgarian and Romanian migration to the UK', Part of Migration Statistics Quarterly Report, 27 August 2015. http://www.ons.gov.uk/ons/rel/migration1/migration-statistics-quarterly-report/august-2015/sty-bulgarian-and-romanian-migration-to-the-uk.html.

10 The term 'higher professional' here covers all forms of professional occupation except for 'assistant professional'.

11 Office for National Statistics, 'Labour market statistics summary data tables', Table 8, 18 December 2013. http://www.ons.gov.uk/ons/publications/re-reference-tables.html?edition=tcm%3A77-292276.

Chapter 2

1 Longhi *et al*, p.12.

2 Borjas and Katz (1997), p.62.

3 Card (2001), p.58.

4 Angrist and Kugler (2003), p. F322

5 Jean and Jiménez (2007), paragraph 37.

6 These numbers are derived from the coefficients given in the last two columns of Table 4.1 of Dustmann *et al* (2003).

7 These studies are summarised in MAC (2012), chapter 4 and Devlin *et al* (2014).

8 Nathan does not directly use the immigrant share in his regressions. Instead he uses a measure of diversity. Although correlated with the share of immigrants in an area, this measure is also influenced by inter-area and inter-temporal variations in the local composition of the immigrant population.

9 MAC (2012), paragraph 4.36.

10 The output gap is the difference between actual GDP and potential GDP. The gap is taken as an indicator of how much slack there is in the economy. A positive gap is associated with a strong

demand for labour and a negative gap with a weak demand for labour.

11 MAC (2012), paragraph 4.33.

12 MAC (2012), paragraph 4.31.

13 MAC (2012), paragraph A.44. This paragraph refers to estimates presented in panel 4 of table A4. The coefficients for non-EU and EU migrants for 1995-2010 are -0.230 (0.003) and -0.238 (0.206) respectively. The numbers in parentheses are p-values. With these p-values it is reasonable to assume that the two coefficients are equal.

14 The relevant regression results are reported in the final column of Table 1 in Annexe 1 of Devlin *et al* (2014). The coefficients for non-EU and EU migrants for 1995-2012 are -0.210 (0.001) and -0.211 (0.225). The numbers in parentheses are p-values.

15 (Devlin *et al*, 2014, p.4):

16 For a summary of the evidence on average wages see Table 4.2 of MAC (2012).

18 These numbers are derived as follows: 5.3 × 0.2 = 1.1 and 5.3 × 0.3 = 1.6.

17 This figure is derived by comparing net migration and population growth under the low and high migration projections.

Chapter 3

1 See Table 1.2.

2 A comparison of the ONS low migration, principal and high migration projections indicates that differences in population between these projections are almost exactly proportional to differences in the assumed rates of net migration. From this property the very low migration projection is derived by linear extrapolation from the ONS low migration projection using the following simple formula:

$$P_{verylow}(x,t) = P_{low}(x,t) - (P_{principal}(x,t) - P_{low}(x,t)) \times 55/60$$

where $P_{verylow}(x,t)$, $P_{principal}(x,t)$ and $P_{low}(x,t)$ are, respectively, the population of age x at time t under the very low migration, principal and low migration projections.

3 The 2012-based UN medium variant population projection for Germany is 76.0 million in 2041, and 71.3 million in 2053. The ONS projects a population for the UK of 76.5 million in 2041 under the high migration scenario. With very low migration the UK population is 71.8 million in 2053. Per capita income is currently somewhat higher in Germany than the UK (11% gap in 2011). However, this gap is likely to close as German society ages

and the share of working age population declines faster than in the UK. This suggests that the UK will overtake Germany in terms of GDP at roughly the same time it does so in terms of population.

4 https://www.gov.uk/government/uploads/system/uploads/attachment_data/file/224894/top-10-crowded-autumn-2012.pdf.

5 Department for Transport, 'Highways Agency motorways and 'A' roads: on-time journeys', 12 December 2013, Table CGN0104.

6 Environment Agency (2008), p.6.

7 For an extensive discussion of the issues involved see Rowthorn (2008).

Chapter 4

1 Equal burden sharing may conflict with the principle that individuals should be taxed in accordance with their ability to pay. This is the principle that underlies the present tax and benefit system. According to this principle, poor migrants should not have to pay their full share of government expenditure because they cannot afford to. It is being increasingly argued that this alternative principle of fairness should only apply to the native population or to long-established immigrants, and not to recent arrivals.

2 Children under 16 years of age who are born in the UK to immigrant parents are classified as immigrants. On reaching 16 they are reclassified as UK natives. This helps to explain why there is a sharp fall in later years in the population of pre-2001 non-EEA migrants.

3 D&F do not give separate figures for pre-2001 migrants. These are derived by subtracting the series for post-2000 migrants from the corresponding series for all migrants.

4 Some of the figures in this table differ very slightly from those given by D&F. This is presumably because I have used a slightly different GDP deflator to convert them to 2011 prices.

5 Some of the points made in the Migration Watch critique were previously made by Nigel Williams (2013) and Mervyn Stone (2013). Stone's paper contains a trenchant critique of D&F's use of probability models to determine the extent to which immigrants from different groups are more or less likely than natives to receive state benefits/tax credits or live in social housing. In their response, D&F (2014a) acknowledge Stone's critique of their probability models, but do not directly address his concerns on this issue.

6 The figure of £462 billion is from D&F Table 4a. Table 4b gives a slightly higher figure of £464 billion. All labour displacement adjustments are based on Table 4a.

7 This range was derived from the benefit calculator on the website of the organisation 'entitled to' (http://www.entitledto.co.uk/). It refers to a single adult without children and annual earnings of £13,125, who is living in a house with council tax band A in Coventry (post code CV5 6FG). The employer's national insurance payment is calculated using the rates given on the government website. For an adult over 25 in rented accommodation with shared facilities the exact fiscal loss is £9,194 excluding indirect taxes. For an adult of 23 living with parents the fiscal loss is £4,368 excluding indirect taxes.

8 The method used to assign government interest payments is described in Appendix 1.

9 OBR (2013), chart A9, p. 147. The OBR estimates are based on the ONS 2010-based population projections.

10 For example, Dorling (2013).

11 The fiscal gain is derived by comparing the high migration and central projections in OBR (2015), Table 5.1, p. 117. Note that the population projections in the OBR report are the same as the ONS 2012-based projections.

12 OBR (2015), paragraph 3.104.

Conclusions

1 'David Cameron: net immigration will be capped at tens of thousands', *The Daily Telegraph*, 10 January, 2010.

2 Citizens of Iceland, Liechtenstein, Norway and Switzerland enjoy the same rights of entry to the UK as do EU citizens.

3 For a discussion of the regulations governing labour movement within the EU and the possibility of reform see Booth *et al* (2012).

4 'Britain will not stop EU migrants coming here to work, says Cameron', *The Daily Telegraph*, 12 May 2014.

5 IMF WEO database, April 2015. www.imf.org/external/pubs/ft/weo/2015/01/weodata/index.aspx

6 David Cameron, 'Free movement within Europe needs to be less free', *Financial Times*, 26 November 2013.

7 'I'll veto new EU states unless we deal with mass migration, pledges David Cameron', *The Daily Telegraph*, 20 December 2013.

8 Some of the issues raised in this section are discussed at length in Parts 4 and 5 of Paul Collier's book *Exodus* (Collier, 2013).

9 OECD, 'Is this humanitarian migration crisis different?', Migration Policy Debates, September 2015, Table 1.

10 UN zero migration projections for the total population of Sub-Saharan Africa are as follows: 962 millon (2015) and 2,142 million (2050), 3,985 million (2100). Source: http://esa.un.org/unpd/wpp/DVD/

11 Rodrik (2011), pp. 268-272.

12 The issue of migrant rights is discussed at length in Ruhs (2013).

13 For a good survey of this topic see Gibson & McKenzie (2011).

14 James Fontanella-Khan, 'Romanians despair that wealthy Britain is taking all their doctors', Financial Times, 14 January 2014. Note that the total number of Romanian doctors (including locums) working in the NHS in September 2013 was 477, which is less than one tenth of the doctors who apparently left Romania during the period 2011-2013.

15 Extract from Article 1 A(2) of the UN Convention as modified by the 1967 Protocol.

16 All numbers in this paragraph are from Eurostat: http://ec.europa.eu/eurostat/statistics-explained/images/f/f2/First_instance_decisions_by_outcome_and_recognition_rates%2C_2nd_quarter_2015.png

17 Open Europe, '200,000 asylum seekers arrive in Germany in September as Interior Minister pushes for EU-wide "refugee cap"', Blog, 1 October 2015.

18 'UK to accept 20,000 refugees from Syria by 2020', BBC News website, 7 September 2015.

19 'Britain faces £150m cost for EU migrant crisis', *The Daily Telegraph*, 23 September 2015.

20 Open Europe, '200,000 asylum seekers arrive in Germany in September as Interior Minister pushes for EU-wide "refugee cap"', Blog, 1 October 2015.

21 OECD, Is this humanitarian migration crisis different?', Migration Policy Debates, September 2015, Table 1. See also Cebulla *et al* (2010)

22 OECD, Is this humanitarian migration crisis different?', Migration Policy Debates, September 2015, Table 1.

23 See article 1 C(5) of the UN Convention on Refugees.